The Way of the Cross

Going From Death to Life

Judah Veritas

This book is dedicated to all the martyrs of the faith who endured to the very end.

""Whoever desires to come after Me, let him deny himself, and take up his cross, and follow Me. For whoever desires to save his life will lose it, but whoever loses his life for My sake and the gospel's will save it.""

— *Mark 8:34-35*

Contents

Preface

♦

"We pray for our enemies; we seek to persuade those who hate us without cause to live conformably to the goodly precepts of Christ, that they may become partakers with us of the joyful hope of blessings from God, the Lord of all." Justin Martyr

This book was written to better understand what Christ did upon the Cross and how it should affect our lifestyle. Without understanding the Cross, we labor in vain. Without doing as God commands and truly living in light of the Cross of Christ, we shall forever miss the mark.

God, in His Divine Sovereignty, has allowed us to know Him through Christ and what was done on the Cross. It is only by God that we can live for God. In understanding what Christ did, we can better live. In knowing **The Way of the Cross**, we can live through the Cross.

It is important to briefly note that the "Cross" of Christ is capitalized to emphasize the Cross, but it is not meant to be worshipped or idolized. Christ is the only One we are to worship.

After each chapter is "Quotes for Meditation". These range in depth from certain denominational Christians, old Catholics, puritans, and other mighty saints of God. All quotes are meant to gain a deeper understanding of the Cross through meditation. For at the Cross is an unfolding amount of revelation to be found, grasped, and understood.

The pages in this book are meant to grow in God, understand what happened on the Cross, and what we are to do about it. Without understanding the Cross, living a crucified life will be near impossible. Without understanding the stages of what leads a man to die, he shall never find life.

May God draw the hearts of men and women closer to Him through the pages of this book.

Introduction

"The Cross not only shows the love of God more gloriously than anything else—it also shows His righteousness, His justice, His holiness, and all the glory of His eternal attributes. They are all to be seen shining together there." Martyn Lloyd-Jones

The Cross is a holy symbol that signifies God, Life, and change through death. It reveals the attributes of God while at the same time showing the path to living for God.

Without understanding the Cross, we shall never fully press into the mark of Jesus Christ. Without knowing *The Way of the Cross*, we shall forever miss the mark on what God desires to do through us.

Those who are unwilling to change shall forever remain enslaved. The only path for a Christian is to die. Die to himself, his ways, ambitions, goals, and dreams. By dying to self, we can then take up what is of God. There may be similarities between God's Vision and what we thought our life would be, but only when we die can we carry out that vision with a pure heart.

Without the willingness to die and seek change, a man shall forever fall short of being what God desires that man to be.

We must first understand that the path to death is a long and lonely road. Few there be who endure to the end. Few are willing to walk down the road less traveled. For the cross is heavy. Yet, sin is heavier. If we are unwilling to die to self and sin, we shall never come to know Him.

The path of the Savior is our path. The way of the Lord is our way. We shall only receive glory through suffering for the sake of Christ. We shall only gain Eternal Life when we are willing to die.

God's Way is paradoxical. It is that which man would not do nor would think of. God's Way is the Only Way, and few are willing to take this path. Those who do, however, shall never be put to shame, abandoned, or left alone.

God's Power fuses into the soul who trusts in Him, believe in His promises, understands what Christ did, and possesses a heart that desires to walk in like manner.

Therefore, *The Way of the Cross* consists of six stages:
1) To the Cross
2) At the Cross
3) Hoisting the Cross
4) On the Cross
5) Through the Cross
6) Taking Up Our God-Appointed Cross

This is how a man might not only be saved but live a life that shall receive recognition and reward on that Final Day — not because of our works or merit but because of our submission and surrender to God. By giving all, we are and all that we have to God, God can reign within. By submitting our will to the Holy Spirit, we can bear trials, adversity, and suffering for Him. In exchange, these things will have meaning. They shall not be endured in vain but overcome in the Spirit's power. By suffering for Christ, we can rejoice because our cross is temporal, while the act of Christ upon His Cross was Eternal.

Let us, therefore, look upon the Cross of Christ. Let us not merely gaze upon the beauty of God's work upon the Cross but live in *the Way of the Cross*. For many go *to* the Cross but are not willing to go *through* the Cross. Many arrive *at* the Cross but are not willing to *get on* the Cross. Only those who carry their cross for the glorification of God shall be numbered amongst the saints of God, for it is in the Cross where Power, Love, Renewal, Redemption, Restoration, and Life are found. May we die so that we may live.

* * *

Heavenly Father, we thank You for sending Your Son into the world to die on the Cross for our sins. We thank You that salvation is by Grace through faith. We thank You for loving us so much that You sent Your Son into the world not to condemn the world but to save it. May all repent of their sins and believe in Christ. Please give us the strength and power to endure our cross patiently. May we not lose sight of the hope of eternal salvation. Give us the ability to endure to the end, Holy Spirit. Be our Advocate and Helper. May we bear all things for the sake of Christ, Who loved us and gave up His Life as a ransom for many. May The Cross of Christ be stamped upon our hearts as we take up our cross and follow You, O God. Be glorified and magnified through our lives. May we be holy vessels who endure to the end. May we show mercy and compassion to all, just as You have to us. Give us deeper revelations of the Cross, we pray. In Jesus' name, Amen.

Part One

To The Cross

Chapter 1

To The Cross

"Whoever desires to come after Me, let him deny himself, and take up his cross, and follow Me."
— *The Lord Jesus Christ (Mark 8:34 NKJV)*

There is no other way than by the Cross of Christ. No other decision is more important than taking up our cross and following Christ. This way is painful, lonely, and brutal. It is filled with strife and tears. It is a path that is honest with what will come. It does not seek to hide or deny the hard truth that a cross is painful.

A cross draws the eyes of all, but very few will go in the way of the Cross. Very few are willing to deny themselves. Very few are ready to place Jesus Christ as Lord and Savior.

As we venture to the Cross, we must strip away what is keeping us from the Love of God, the Wisdom of God, and the Righteousness of God. Whatever does not pertain to God or is not of God must die.

As we take up all the baggage we have been carrying; we

take it to a destination. We no longer want to put on a façade or disguise ourselves from what is happening. For reality is not merely that which is physical but what is metaphysical. The components of our inner life will be exposed and seen for what they are.

We will feel the weight of our sin. We will be brought to our knees by Holy Ghost conviction. In the end, however, our final state will be blessed. "The end of a thing *is* better than its beginning; The patient in spirit *is* better than the proud in spirit" (Ecclesiastes 7:8 NKJV).

As we patiently endure the road ahead of going to the cross, we shall learn that it is a road less traveled. We shall be mocked and ridiculed. We shall be slandered as we take this lonely road. However, we are not going to die with the crowd. Instead, we choose to die with Christ to be raised with Christ. From death to life. This is the way, beginning with making our way to the Cross.

Chapter 2

A Conscious Decision

"" **A**nd *he who does not take his cross and follow after Me is not worthy of Me.""* Matthew 10:38 NKJV

When a man or woman chooses to take up their cross for Christ, they shall never return the same. When a conscious decision is made to move toward the path of death, we can expect loneliness, abandonment, and persecution.

For those who carry a cross carry more than a symbol. They carry a way of life that will be both forgotten and forsaken. As they make their way to be crucified, they consciously have chosen to die to that which has kept them in captivity. They acknowledge they have been guilty of sin and are wicked before God. However, their desire to take up their cross is due to the glory that awaits after their death.

When a decision is made to take up our cross and head to the Cross, there are bound to be opinions. These opinions can come even from those who are closest to us.

When we love others and know that they love us, they will often indirectly attempt to withhold us from going further. They become either intimidated or afraid of what might happen.

Friends might become fearful that our decision is the right one. If it is, they are in the wrong to talk us out of that situation. They attempt to talk us out of taking up our cross because they don't want to be the only ones to fall short of what they are called to do. They don't want to be solely responsible for neglecting what needs to be done.

Rather than being loving friends, they become selfish friends. That which they must die to, they overindulge in. Rather than supporting a person's decision to follow Christ, they attempt to drag them down. They seek to keep them in their iniquity or lazy lifestyle. This is because the friend does not want to change and therefore does not want the other person to change. They want to keep things as they are. If they themselves are to go down, they would rather go down with company than on their own.

The person who consciously decides to choose the way of the cross decides to go on their own and not with the crowd. They are making a decision that is a one-way direction. Once the cross is taken up, there is no going back. Once the decision has been made, there is both a responsibility and a burden that lies ahead. The responsibility is in following through with what one has chosen to do. The burden is leaving behind that which was familiar and comfortable.

Any man or woman who chooses the way of the cross shall be uncomfortable. They shall go into unknown territory. Trials and adversity that could have otherwise been prevented will occur. For Christ promises ""In the world you will have tribulation; but be of good cheer, I have overcome the world"" (John 16:33 NKJV).

If we choose Christ, we choose the path to life. However, true life can only occur through death. Truly, the Christian way of life is a paradoxical life. If we desire to be raised up, we must humble ourselves. If we want everlasting life, we must die to sin and self. God's ways are not our ways and His thoughts are not our thoughts. God made a beautiful story through the Cross, and the Cross helps to reveal those who are committed and those who are not. Those who see the Cross of Christ, understand its meaning and what Christ did, and are willing to make a conscious decision to take up their cross shall be truly on the path of saving grace.

God could have made the process *easy*. Though He has made it *simple* to understand, He could have *hypothetically* made it easy (though, He never would have, as that would have been contrary to His nature). He could have said, "simply believe, and that's it! There's no need to die to your sin and self-ishness, which put my Son on the Cross. There is no need to repent of your sins. Just believe!" In God's Divine Wisdom, He knew that the cross was the only way. He knew that the Cross would offend those who believed they could earn their salvation any other way than through Christ.

Though we are called to live a life of repentance, this follows after true faith. When we first repent, we reveal what we believe. When we truly believe, we receive the Holy Spirit. When we have the Holy Spirit, He shall forever convict us and lead us to repentance when we are wrong. "Or do you despise the riches of His goodness, forbearance, and longsuffering, not knowing that the goodness of God leads you to repentance?" (Romans 2:4 NKJV). It is out of God's kindness and goodness that we are led to repentance, for the Cross is both a symbol and a lifestyle.

If those who want to play the game of religion neglect the One, True God as the Sole Source of all things (including their salvation), they shall receive destruction. For the Cross directly confronts the sinner. It says that we are responsible for sending Christ to the Cross.

We are to follow our Lord and Savior if we are to genuinely live for Him. We are commanded to die. For a Cross signifies testing, trial, and torture. The testing comes from who will truly go to the cross and die upon it. The trial comes from refusing to give in to the voices that would otherwise tempt us away from the path God demands us to take. The torture comes from the painful death of dying to our selfish motives, desires, sinful passions, and other ways that spit in the face of God. To die to these things, though it appears terrible in the beginning, leads towards a glorious ending.

By making this decision, we learn that the way to life is through death. When we consciously acknowledge the road before us, we can take up our cross, knowing its burden will soon lift. The weight and pain of our sin shall quickly cease. We will become new creatures once our old man is put to death.

This is the beauty in the one chosen to be a true born-again believer. God calls all to Him (1 Timothy 2:4, 2 Peter 3:9). However, only some respond and accept that call. Therefore, God only chooses some based on the authenticity of their response. For a man can admire the Cross of Christ from afar. However, it takes courage and humility to go in the way of the Cross. It takes a broken and contrite heart to know the love of Christ upon that Cross and be willing to give our all back to Him. For without Him, we are nothing and have nothing. With Him, we have everything.

""For what will it profit a man if he gains the whole world, and loses his own soul? Or what will a man give in exchange for his soul?"" (Mark 8:36-37 NKJV). What can a man have, obtain, or give in exchange for his soul? This is the question to be meditated upon. All the riches in the world will not save a man.

"A rich man's wealth is his strong city, and like a high wall in his imagination" (Proverbs 18:11 ESV). All the material possessions, resources, and connections in this life cannot save a man from eternal damnation. It is only Christ. If we are to be saved by what Christ has done, we must live the way of Christ. If we are to live in the Truth of what Christ did, we must obey Him, take up our cross, and follow Him.

This initial beginning starts within the heart. It is a disposition set upon God and nothing else. If the mind is willing to acknowledge the heart's conviction, it shall forever keep its eyes gazing in His direction. One must first recognize the crucified Christ to see and live with the risen Christ. Without acknowledging what Christ did and why He did it, we shall merely gaze upon the Hill of Golgotha and turn from it—for mental ascent never led a man to truly repent. Only by way of the mind and heart confirming what Christ has done will one consciously choose the path of the crucified life.

If we are to truly know the One, True Christ, then we will follow in His footsteps. We will go in a similar way to the cross. We will understand the long and lonely road that leads to death. By doing so, we shall understand the beauty of God's redemptive and restorative work. We shall be living vessels covered by the Blood as we receive the promised hope of eternal life with God. This only comes through death.

Being willing to die starts with a broken and contrite heart, followed by a conscious decision. Not only to gaze and acknowledge Christ from afar but to take up our cross and make our way to Him.

* * *

Triune God, You are the God of Truth. You are the God of Love Who is Holy and dwells in Unapproachable Light. O God, may we not find it strange when You call us to die. May we not argue our way out of the true path of a born-again believer. God, we are guilty before You. We are sinners in need of Your saving Grace and restorative Power! God in Heaven, we repent of our sin before You. We acknowledge that we stand before You guilty, apart from Christ. It is only by Grace through faith we are saved. It is only through Christ that we can come to know You, Heavenly Father. God, we ask for Your forgiveness and Your power. Forgive us of our sins and give us the power of the Holy Spirit to walk in the way You are commanding us to go in. May we not succumb to our fleshly wants and only go halfway. Give us the humility to recognize we are the ones who sent Christ to the Cross. Give us the courage to take up our cross and follow You. For the path of salvation can only come by way of crucifixion. Be glorified, O God, as we submit and surrender our all to You. In Jesus' name, Amen.

Quotes For Meditation

1. "Consider the end of life and you will love nothing in this world." **St. Laurence Justinian**
2. "We are bid to take, not to make our cross." **William Gurnall**
3. "O wretched slaves of Mammon, you cannot glory in the Cross of our Lord Jesus Christ while you trust in treasures laid up on earth: you cannot taste and see how gracious the Lord is, while you are hungering for gold." **Bernard of Calirvaux**
4. The Lord calls to Himself all sinners; He opens His arms wide, even to the worst among them. He takes them all in His arms, if only they will come." **John Chrysostom**
5. "The man with a cross no longer controls his destiny; he lost control when he picked up his cross. That cross immediately became to him an all-absorbing interest, an overwhelming interference. No matter what he may desire to do, there is but

one thing he can do; that is, move on toward the place of crucifixion." **A.W. Tozer**

Chapter 3

The Road Less Traveled

"Now may the Lord direct your hearts into the love of God and into the patience of Christ." *2 Thessalonians 3:5 NKJV*

Ego inflates and deceives.

Many times we are not real with ourselves. We cover up sins. We seek to excuse that which we do because we "deserve to" or "have the right". We think we are well on our way to establishing our own utopian end when we are simply heaping upon ourselves destruction.

Speak to the average person about the Cross; they will know little. They will see it as a means by which they are saved while thinking they can still be enslaved to their sinful ways and lifestyles. Little do they know that God calls and demands us to die. This death comes by way of walking down the road less traveled.

Few are willing to walk before men and women carrying a

cross. Few can march on past others' opinions, perceptions, and slander.

When a conscious decision is made to follow Christ, God draws our hearts to Him. He gives us the strength to walk the road less traveled. Though most may be religious to some degree, many are unwilling to allow God to destroy them of themselves. Not destroy, as in annihilate or put to a literal, physical death. Rather, destroy ego, self, and carnal ambition. "For where envy and self-seeking *exist,* confusion and every evil thing *are* there" (James 3:16 NKJV).

Religion that brings forth self-seeking is not one worth following or leading. It is deceptive and boosts man's ego rather than exalts God. Anyone who exalts God prostrates before Him. Anyone who lifts the Name of God is brought low. Anyone who puts God first is both humble and humbled. A person who does not partake in these things knows not the One, True God. They have created a man-made "god" where whatever their "god" says is permitted.

The difference between following the God of the Word and the god of the mind is that the former conforms and bends their will to Christ, rather than having their god conform to their wants and ideology. For anything that conforms to man is not god. However, anything that conforms to Christ will surely be refined as gold is refined by fire. There will be a humbling and a surrendering. The rise out of the fire shall bring forth a new, purified creature.

Therefore, we must understand the patience of Christ. For Christ went through the worst form of torture and torment. He was so wounded that another man had to carry His cross on His behalf. "Now as they came out, they found a man of Cyrene, Simon by name. Him they compelled to bear His cross" (Matthew 27:32 NKJV).

When we carry our cross, we don't need help from another

man. We are solely responsible for taking up our cross because the weight of our cross is minute in comparison to Christ's. What we think is difficult and too strenuous is exceptionally light for Christ to bear.

God promises to go before us and help us bear the weight of our burdens. He commands us to cast our anxieties on Him because He cares for us (1 Peter 5:7). However, we cannot cast anything upon Christ until we are found in Christ. This road to the Cross is one only we can take for ourselves. God calls us, but He does not give us the power or strength until we die. Until we fully submit to Him, we are tested on this road. Our faith is proven based on our willingness or unwillingness to die.

Those who go halfway to the cross do not get on the cross. They depart because it is "too hard" or "unbearable". Though appearances may seem one has gone all the way, that is not what is reality. The path is the testing ground. Without listening to the call to head towards the hill to which we are to be crucified, we shall have a weak faith. For any faith that does not command one to give all to God shall not receive the strength and power of God.

Those who trust more in the hardship of the way than in God's deliverance or God's Sovereignty will forever live with the idol of externals. For anyone who believes that situations and circumstances are above God have chosen to submit to that which only God can control. They wield a blinded view of God. The mind becomes clouded by what it perceives rather than having child-like belief in Him Who created all things, knows all things, loves all things, and is calling all to Him.

The road to Christ can always be seen. It can be noticed from afar off. It is easy to understand, but many are unwilling to take it. That is why we must not become discouraged when those who appeared to be saved fall away. They are those who could see the Cross of Christ upon the Hill. They could regurgitate and say what Christ has done, but they have not drawn close to Him. They have admired Him from afar but have refused to walk the road they are called to go. Therefore, many people's faith is proven to be a lie or shipwrecked. Many think that knowing what Christ has done or giving mental ascent to what they have heard or seen is enough. This, however, is not enough. A man can *know about* something without *knowing* something.

We can *know about* the 16th President of the United States (Abraham Lincoln) without truly *knowing* him. This is the case for many so-called believers. Many know about Christ. Many know what Christ has done, but to draw near and truly understand, experience, and know Him is far from reality. This is because they have refused to take up their cross and deny themselves. They have refused to follow Christ and therefore exalted themselves and placed ease, comfort, and other temporary aspects above God. These people will hear on that Final Day, ""Depart from Me, you cursed, into the everlasting fire prepared for the devil and his angels'" (Matthew 25:41 NKJV).

God calls us to follow in the way of Christ, and this can only come with fully submerging in what He has done. We cannot come to know Christ truly if we will not truly walk down the road in which He went. Though the path is similar and leads to a common end, Christ's was infinitely more painful and excruciating. If we cannot understand this reality, we will think our path is equally difficult.

Though our path will not be easy, it is not at all in the same manifestation of hardship as Christ. None of us could take on the full weight of sin, remain perfect and patient, and humbly endure the torture and torment Christ went through.

When we begin to be realistic with what God commands of us, we can more readily endure what lies ahead. Though our death will be painful, it will not be forever. Glory is on the other side, but first we must walk the road leading to death. Death of self. Death of sin. Death of pleasing others. Death of living how we want. By this death, God then gives us His power. He gives us His vision.

This death is not one that does not guarantee a better life on the other side. The newness of life given by God is glorious. Meaning and purpose are bestowed upon the faithful followers of Christ. Transformation takes place, and we become holy vessels who are the temples of Him, the Holy Light of Christ. The Holy Spirit resides in us, and we no longer live in darkness, but as children of God. "You are all sons of light and sons of the day. We are not of the night nor of darkness" (1 Thessalonians 5:5 NKJV). This is promised to those who walk down the road that leads to both death and life.

Taking up our cross automatically recognizes that we have been in the wrong. We are guilty before God, and there is no other way than to reveal to God that we desire His Mercy, His forgiveness, His Grace, and His Love. He is more willing to give than we are to receive, and nothing worth receiving comes easy. Nothing worth obtaining and acquiring comes automatically. All things require work and sacrifice.

Though salvation is free and is by grace through faith (Ephesians 2:8-9), it does require sacrifice on our end. If we are not willing to sacrifice that which our flesh desires and place ourselves upon the altar and die, we shall not receive the Holy Spirit.

The Holy Spirit is the only One who can make us Holy. There is no other way but to sacrifice all we want and all we have come to know apart from Christ, and believe in Him with childlike faith and surrender.

May God give us the courage to go down the road less traveled so that we may gain what is offered to all, but which few receive.

Judah Veritas

Glory be to God for the Cross of Christ.

* * *

Triune God, we thank You for providing the way to salvation. We are sinners in need of a Savior. We come before You, the Absolute Supreme One, Who is Holy, Holy, Holy, and we seek Thee for Thy strength and power. O God, may we commit to the way You call us to go. May we surrender all to You and take up all from You. For Your ways are higher than our ways. Your blessings are greater than worldly possessions. O God, may we deny ourselves daily and take up our cross. May the weight and burden of our sin and selfishness be taken from our backs. As we kneel before You, Him Who is Righteous, Pure, and Perfect, may You touch us with Thy Divine Love. Captivate our hearts and minds. Renew and restore us. We bless Your Holy Name. In Jesus' name, Amen.

Quotes For Meditation

1. "Christ went more willingly to the cross than we do to the throne of grace." **Thomas Watson**
2. "If my preaching of this Cross is not an offense to the natural man, I am misrepresenting it." **Martyn Lloyd-Jones**
3. "Carrying the cross does mean following in Jesus' footsteps. And in His footsteps are rejection, brokenheartedness, persecution and death. There are not two Christs - an easy going one for easy going Christians, and a suffering one for exceptional believers. There is only one Christ. Are we willing to follow His lead?" **Hudson Taylor**
4. "The way of the cross is the way of suffering. Christians are called to die, not kill, in order to show the world how they are loved by Christ." **John Piper**
5. "True love goes ever straight forward, not in its own strength, but esteeming itself as nothing. Then

indeed we are truly happy. The cross is no longer a cross when there is no self to suffer under it."
Francois Fenelon

Chapter 4

A Lonely Walk

"H*e will not be afraid of evil tidings; His heart is steadfast, trusting in the Lord."* Psalm 112:7 NKJV

Our walk to the Cross is lonely, but it does not mean we are alone. Though we may feel that everyone has abandoned us and is against us, God is with us. He gives us the encouragement and strength to walk on the path many are unwilling to go. He gives us the blessed truth of knowing that the end of what is to come is filled with peace, joy, transformation, and excitement. Though this walk is scary and frightening, its end leads toward something that cannot be obtained otherwise.

Sometimes the most profitable way is the most painful way — not through self-inflicted pain, but through a willingness to move forward. To take on adversity is one of the most beautiful sights known to man. For someone to face the troubling times and allow God to guide them to the end is a life worth admiring and living.

We need not merely admire what Christ has done from afar. Instead, we must draw nigh to Him. We must walk in His footsteps as He walks beside us. "Draw near to God and He will draw near to you. Cleanse *your* hands, *you* sinners; and purify *your* hearts, *you* double-minded. Lament and mourn and weep! Let your laughter be turned to mourning and *your* joy to gloom. Humble yourselves in the sight of the Lord, and He will lift you up" (James 4:8-10 NKJV).

When we draw near to God, He will draw near to us. This drawing is at the foot of the Cross. If we are unwilling to endure the lonely walk and take up our Cross, we shall never draw near to Him, Who created all things. We shall never have Christ, Who bore our sins, draw near to us.

To grow closer to God, we must go in the way of God. We must be willing to look past the temporal present and look to the eternal future. We must ignore the deafening silence of our lonely walk and hear angels rejoicing. ""Likewise, I say to you, there is joy in the presence of the angels of God over one sinner who repents"" (Luke 15:10 NKJV).

Our walk resembles the truthfulness of our faith. Faith is active. Faith is not merely an acknowledgment but a lifestyle. When we choose Christ, we choose to die to self. We want Him to be our All in All. As we become nothing, He becomes everything.

When we choose to humble ourselves before God Almighty, people will misunderstand our pursuit. They will mock and ridicule us. Friendships that we thought were strong will be proven weak and superficial. Who we thought would be there with us all along are those who quickly abandon us. For those who choose the path of holiness will be abandoned by others.

Not everyone will endure the lonely walk. Instead of going to the Cross, many will stay behind. They will indulge in their drink, food, and pleasure. They will cease wanting to be changed. They will be those who hate conviction and want everything to do with comfort, ease, and agreement with how they live.

Sadly, this is the state of many around those who choose otherwise. For to make a painful decision is to go against the grain immediately. It is not going with the tide. Instead, it is swimming against the stream.

To choose to go towards the hill where we shall die is no easy feat. It is not for the weak in heart. It is not for the self-deceived. It is not for those who are afraid or fearful. Instead, it is for those who possess the wings of courage and humility. It is for those who are not afraid of dying to gain newness of life. It is for those humble enough to recognize they are sinners and need something outside of themselves to save them from themselves. This is the way of the Cross of Christ.

"Beware lest anyone cheat you through philosophy and empty deceit, according to the tradition of men, according to the basic principles of the world, and not according to Christ. For in Him dwells all the fullness of the Godhead bodily; and you are complete in Him, Who is the head of all principality and power" (Colossians 2:8 NKJV). There is no other way but the way of the Cross. There is no one else then Christ, Whom we are to mimic and imitate. If Christ endured the lonely road and was willing to be forsaken by His Father, how much more should we take up our cross and follow Him?

The abandonment of the world always brings forth initial shock and distress. We will be questioned why we are doing what we are doing. The vocals from others and the actions they do to us will be harmful and hurtful. Though they may know what they do, they also do not know what they do.

When others are allowed to mock and ridicule us, it offers a testing ground if we truly are sold out for Christ. When people are allowed by God to do and say offensive things, we must remember that they do so because the Cross is offensive. The Cross of Christ is a blessing and a beautiful sight. However, to all, at some point or another, it is an offense. It declares that we are not good. It reveals that we are sinners and there is no other way but by the Cross that men might be saved. Not merely to It, but through It; and we can only go through It, when we believe in Him Who hung upon It. Glory be to God for His willingness to do what is undeserved and should not have been done! Praise God for both the death and resurrection of the King of kings and Lord of lords!

Dear friend, do not fear when the walk is lonely. Those who see another carrying a cross immediately focus on that person's sins while wholly neglecting their own. They will mock from afar. As we get closer to the hill by which we shall be crucified, others will watch from a distance. Some will walk away from us merely to indulge in their godlessness. Most, however, will go but a few steps with us.

We shall walk down the path by ourselves in the physical realm, but we are never alone in the spiritual. Our end does not lead to living for damnation. Instead, it leads to everlasting life through death. This is the only way by which men might be saved. It is to follow in the Way and believe in Him Who paved the Way.

When we choose to take up our cross, we shall never return to our old ways, habits, lifestyle, and friends that want nothing to do with God. It is both lonely and difficult to leave all we have ever known. Like one moving from their hometown for thirty years to a new city, so is it on the path of becoming born again.

Transformation will take place, and it won't be easy. It will seem like nobody is for us. Yet, we must remember that "If God *is* for us, who *can be* against us?" (Romans 8:31

NKJV). He will not leave us stranded. He will speak and walk beside us as we go to the Cross. In dying, He will give us His Holy Spirit. Through this, we shall die from our old selves and live in the new. "Therefore, if anyone *is* in Christ, *he is* a new creation; old things have passed away; behold, all things have become new" (2 Corinthians 5:17 NKJV).

Old things can only pass away if we seek to put them away. They shall continue to hold onto us if we continue to hold onto them. We must have enough desire for God and enough volition to walk straight ahead to where we must die. We must have the willingness to surrender all before God. People's opinions, doubts, shame, and guilt are on this path. We will find restoration when we are humble enough to recognize that our sin put Christ upon the Cross; when we are courageous enough not to hide anything, but to be exposed by the Light. It is a lonely walk when a man is headed to die. However, that man shall never be alone.

The Love and Truth of God lead us to the Cross. It exposes us to what we are and reveals what we can be. Anything worth taking up involves the cost of laying other things down. Will we endure this lonely walk by which no one can force us? Will we have the capacity and capability to complete the walk before us? Time shall reveal if we are truly sold out for Him Who loves us and died for us.

"For the love of Christ compels us, because we judge thus: that if One died for all, then all died; and He died for all, that those who live should live no longer for themselves, but for Him Who died for them and rose again" (2 Corinthians 5:14-15 NKJV). May our cross be seen as easy to bear because we do not take it alone. God is on the Throne and the One Who will help us carry our cross to the very end.

Even if it seems unbearable, He will give us the strength to persevere. For God is more than willing. The question is, are we?

* * *

God of All, Who existed before time began and is the Author and Finisher of our faith, direct our steps. Give us the courage to turn from the crowd and turn towards You. Give us the strength to endure and press on to the very end. Bless us, O God, with humility to deny ourselves. God, we shall not be afraid of evil tidings, for we are remaining steadfast in the pursuit of You. Holy Spirit, help us never quit or surrender to the crowds or Enemy. If we are to be lonely in this life, may we know that we are never alone. You are with us. Your Rod and Your Staff comfort us. Help us walk the Way You have called us to go. May You Who began a good work in us reveal Thy faithfulness in completing it to the very end. Be Magnified and Glorified, O God our salvation. In Jesus' name, Amen.

Quotes For Meditation

1. "The weightiest end of the cross of Christ that is laid upon you, lieth upon your strong Savior." **Samuel Rutherford**

2. "The cross of Christ is the sweetest burden that I ever bore; it is such a burden as wings are to a bird, or sails to a ship, to carry me forward to my harbor." **Samuel Rutherford**

3. "He who calls us, came here below, to give us the means of getting there. He chose the wood that would enable us to cross the sea – indeed, no-one can Cross the ocean of this world, who is not borne by the Cross of Christ. Even the blind can cling to this Cross. If you can't see where you are going very well, don't let go of it, it will guide you by itself." **St. Augustine**

4. "We know one thing about a man who leaves with a cross, he isn't coming back." **Leonard Ravenhill**

5. "The Cross is the way to Paradise, but only when it is borne willingly." **Paul of the Cross**

Chapter 5

Hated & Ridiculed

"**B**ut you have carefully followed my doctrine, manner of life, purpose, faith, longsuffering, love, perseverance, persecutions, afflictions, which happened to me at Antioch, at Iconium, at Lystra—what persecutions I endured. And out of them all the Lord delivered me. Yes, and all who desire to live godly in Christ Jesus will suffer persecution."
2 Timothy 3:10-12 NKJV

The Christian Road is true and honest. It is filled with the realities of life.

If we follow Christ, we are to be hated and ridiculed. We will be persecuted on all sides and in all ways. We will be misunderstood by those both outside and inside the church. There will be times of anger, resentment, and hatred towards us. People will not want to hear what we say, let alone change their way of living.

Though the words we offer to them are the Bread of Life, they will want nothing to do with It. Although we speak the

Word which edifies, builds up, convicts, and encourages, man would rather live in darkness than Light. This is because their deeds are evil (John 3:19).

Light brings conviction and reveals what is and should be. Darkness attempts to conceal what is done and desires that it will not be discovered. This battle between what is of God and what is not of God is the ongoing battle between the Spirit and the flesh. It will forever occur, so long as we are here in this life and until the Lord's return.

There are no detours when we go in the narrow way that leads to eternal life. When one carries their cross to the Hill to be crucified, they cannot seek a different path. For each detour is blocked by those who are of the world. Each side path has groups of people ready and willing to mock us. They will accuse us of all sorts of things. They will hate us because we are deemed as having done wrong, which we have, but not in the way they presume.

What God declares is wrong, the world accepts as good. "Consider the work of God; For who can make straight what He has made crooked?" (Ecclesiastes 3:17 NKJV). We are guilty as sinners before God. Our crooked ways can never be made straight. Ironically, when a man or woman takes up their cross, they are going down the straight-way. The straight-way is the right way. The crooked way goes astray.

When we take up our cross, we cannot go the crooked way because it is blocked by those who hate us. Where does this hatred come from? Does it come from a clear conscience and a sound mind? No. Only a sound mind can come by the Holy Spirit (2 Timothy 1:7). Those of the world do not possess Him Who is of the Word. Therefore, their hatred and ridicule are not based upon sound judgment but rather a deceptive turning away and lethargic response towards conviction.

This is the battle. Those of the Light want others to see the true Christ through the genuine walk of Christ to the Cross. They want others to comprehend and understand all that Christ has done fully. The world, however, wants nothing to do with God. They immediately hate without warrant. They ridicule without reason. They are led by their carnality and choose to despise the Way that leads to everlasting life. Their viewpoint is not formulated by our misrepresentation of Christ (though this can happen). Instead, it is through a lack of desire to relinquish their rights and fully submit and surrender to God.

The irony is that in surrendering all, we find All. In submitting everything to God, we can take up everything He gives and shall give with the recognition that it comes from Him.

Without humility, a person will never think of going to the Cross. They will forever indulge in their pride and lusts. They will turn from any reproof or correction. "For they are a rebellious people, lying children, children unwilling to hear the instruction of the LORD; who say to the seers, "Do not see," and to the prophets, "Do not prophesy to us what is right; speak to us smooth things, prophesy illusions, leave the way, turn aside from the path, let us hear no more about the Holy One of Israel""" (Isaiah 30:9-11 ESV).

The path of holiness always convicts an ungodly conscience. Those who want nothing to do with the way of Christ will continuously seek to deviate us from the path. This comes in various forms, but hatred and ridicule are one.

Somehow, they find great pleasure in mocking a soon-to-become saint on their way to the Cross. They find great joy in spewing out vehement language. They are quick to speak and slow to listen. They judge based on their own intellect, which is perverse and darkened.

The conversation that "I am done living my way. I choose

God", and the transformation that is about to begin and is already taking place within us convict others that they should do the same. Rather than seeing the blessed state death to self leads to, they quickly harden themselves. They become easily defensive. When a person is headed towards the Cross, there is not only ridicule as one walks past the crowd but also continued gossip.

Did Christ ever stop to rebuke those who hated Him on His way to Golgotha? Did He ever put down His Cross to have a conversation? No. He continued down the path. Silent and without words toward the ungodly. He went His way, knowing that it was the right way. He knew that to complete the Father's Will, He had to continue to move forward. He needed to ignore the opinions of others.

He, as the Perfect God-man, Who was without sin became sin for us. "For He made Him Who knew no sin *to be* sin for us, that we might become the righteousness of God in Him" (2 Corinthians 5:21 NKJV). If Christ, Who was perfect, continued on the way to the Cross, how should we, who are guilty and depraved, respond? Should we become bitter, upset, discouraged, and angry at what people say? Should we seek to defend our name and reputation amongst those who will live an eternity in Hell if they do not repent and turn to Christ?

Those bound to Hell should not faze us. They are beings created in God's image but live as if they had made themselves. If they hate and ridicule us, it is because they continuously feed the depravity within. For there is no end to the godlessness within man. If we are to be hated and ridiculed, let it be for the Truth. Let it be for the way to the Cross, where we shall be transformed and changed.

We are not living for this world but for the world to come. We must not desire to live how we used to live. Drink, premarital sex, the pursuit of wealth and fame, drugs, narcissism, seeking the applause of men... it is all vanity. None of it lasts. None of it gives long-term benefits or pleasure.

If we are hated for doing the right thing and going the right way, may we rejoice, for we are on our way to higher ground. We are no longer drowning in the swamp of sin. Instead, we are pressing on to live for Christ. With each step, we get closer to an authentic, Biblical faith. The Visible Image of God becomes more apparent with each step to the Cross. Revelations begin to fill us. Conviction is before us. We are guilty but see that our guilt, shame, and sin can be forgiven. We see a smile when we look up and draw near to Him Whose Blood drips.

We see God in flesh saying, ""Come to Me, all *you* who labor and are heavy laden, and I will give you rest. Take My yoke upon you and learn from Me, for I am gentle and lowly in heart, and you will find rest for your souls. For My yoke *is* easy and My burden is light"" (Matthew 11:28-30 NKJV). Sin is heavy, but Christ's yoke is easy. The only way for true rest is to be crucified.

In this paradox of dying, we find Life. The weight of sin is lifted off. We begin to enter into blessed fellowship with the Father. We shall be chastised and convicted. We will see that we are guilty and deserve to be hoisted upon the Hill. We do not merely see this, however. We see Christ in our place and know what shall come through our crucifixion.

If we are to be resurrected, we must first die. If we are to be born-again, we must be spiritually crucified. We shall never enter eternal rest if we are unwilling to go through this temporal, painful process.

May we continue in the Way so that others may see us sold out for Him Who loves all and died for all, in hopes that all would turn to Him.

Endure patiently what man says, O Saint. God will repay (Romans 12:19). Do not fear man, but fear God. For this is the beginning of Wisdom (Proverbs 9:10). May we hear the blessed Words of Christ in Matthew 10:28-39 (NKJV) as we prepare to stand At the Cross:

"And do not fear those who kill the body but cannot kill the soul. But rather fear Him who is able to destroy both soul and body in hell. Are not two sparrows sold for a copper coin? And not one of them falls to the ground apart from your Father's will. But the very hairs of your head are all numbered. Do not fear therefore; you are of more value than many sparrows. "Therefore whoever confesses Me before men, him I will also confess before My Father who is in heaven. But whoever denies Me before men, him I will also deny before My Father who is in heaven. "Do not think that I came to bring peace on earth. I did not come to bring peace but a sword. For I have come to 'set a man against his father, a daughter against her mother, and a daughter-in-law against her mother-in-law'; and 'a man's enemies *will be* those of his *own* household.' He who loves father or mother more than Me is not worthy of Me. And he who loves son or daughter more than Me is not worthy of Me. And he who does not take his cross and follow after Me is not worthy of Me. He who finds his life will lose it, and he who loses his life for My sake will find it.'"

* * *

God of Glory, Who is the King and Ruler over the Heavens and earth, You are Him Who gives Life and gives it more abundantly. God, may we seek Thee in all things. May we take up Your yoke, for it is easy when done in the power of the Holy Spirit. Give us the courage to press on and into the Marks of Christ. May we endure the hatred from the world for the sake of Thy Name. Keep us steadfast in the faith and our pursuit of You. Draw us into Thy Love. Hide us under the shadow of Thy Wings. Protect us from the Evil One. Strengthen us in Your Power and conform us to the image of Christ. O God, give us clean hands, a pure heart, and a clear conscience. Help us prepare for death so that we might awaken into newness of life. May the glory to come motivate us to endure the death that is to occur. We die to self, as our sin dies upon You, O Christ. Be Lord and King, not only in Heaven and on earth, but in our hearts. In Jesus' name, Amen.

Quotes For Meditation

1. "Sin's remedy is sacrifice. All the Old Testament sacrifices were shadows of the one, glorious, final, all-sufficient sacrifice Jesus made on our behalf on the Cross." **Derek Prince**
2. "To abandon all, to strip one's self of all, in order to seek and follow Jesus Christ naked to Bethlehem where He was born, naked to the hall where He was scourged, and naked to Calvary where He died on the cross, is so great a mystery that neither the thing nor the knowledge of it, is given to any but through faith in the Son of God." **John Wesley**
3. "It is to the Cross that the Christian is challenged to follow his Master: no path of redemption can make a detour around it." **Hans Urs von Balthasar**
4. "It was Christ Who willingly went to the cross, and it was our sins that took Him there." **Franklin Graham**

5. "The Passion of Christ is the greatest and most stupendous work of Divine Love. The greatest and most overwhelming work of God's love." **Paul of the Cross**

Part Two

At The Cross

Chapter 6

At The Cross

"*Christ was crucified because He would have nothing to do with the crowd (even though He addressed Himself to all). He did not want to form a party, an interest group, a mass movement, but wanted to be what He was, the Truth, which is related to the single individual. Therefore, everyone who will genuinely serve the Truth is by that very fact a martyr. To win a crowd is no art; for that only untruth is needed, nonsense, and a little knowledge of human passions. But no witness to the Truth dares to get involved with the crowd.*"
Soren Kierkegaard

Christ is the Way, the Truth, and the Life, and He has revealed this all to us because all these are Him and provided by Him.

There is no other way than by the way of the Cross. When we stand before the Cross, we will be overwhelmed with many emotions. We will gain an understanding of our wickedness and the Love of God. We will see that we deserve nothing and that in Christ is everything. We will gaze upon the Majesty and

Beauty of the Cross. For when we stand at the Cross, we can see more closely what the crucified life entails.

Many people venture down the path of the cross. Many even make their way to the Cross. However, the deciding factor is whether we will get on the Cross.

Anyone can see a sight and show appreciation. Anyone can enjoy autobiographies and be led to being motivated. If asked, "Would you want to do what they did to get where they got?" the answer would be, most times, "no". Even we are unprepared and unwilling to go in the way of Christ. That is why it takes the Holy Spirit's leading to get us to the point of making our way to the Cross and having the strength to get on the Cross.

The Holy Spirit leads all men to the Cross as He dwells outside our being. For the Holy Spirit to live within, however, we must be crucified. There is no other way. Either we live for self and die, or we die to self and live.

The Holy Spirit guides us every step of the way, but His life-changing and spiritual-transforming power can only enter us when we fully submit to Him.

The symbol of the Cross is "t". This "t" can represent where all Truth may be known, experienced, and found. For if God is Absolute Truth (which He is), all truths flow from Him, whether we recognize it or not.

Let us now stand at the foot of the Cross and gain understanding as to what took place and what must take place within us. May we all find Truth at the Cross.

Chapter 7

Seeing Ourselves for Who We Are

"For many walk, of whom I have told you often, and now tell you even weeping, that they are the enemies of the cross of Christ: whose end is destruction, whose god is their belly, and whose glory is in their shame—who set their mind on earthly things." Philippians 3:18-19 NKJV

We are images of God that desire to be our own god. We seek to serve self and excuse all sin. Naturally, the way of man is wicked. We are not good within ourselves. Sometimes, man may do what is externally good, but internally, we all are dead. We are depraved and need God's Gracious touch and Sovereign Power.

Standing at the Cross, we understand that we sent Christ to the Cross. We see why this Perfect, Innocent Lamb had to be slaughtered for our sake. We begin to process that we would continue down the path of destruction and be damned had Christ not stepped in and taken the full blow of God's wrath. Had Christ chosen not to do so, our hope of salvation would have been diminished. We would have been left to our own understanding and resources, which counts as nothing.

If we are so quick to disappoint and do wrong to our friends and family, how much more are we before a Holy, Just God? Will we truly go to the Cross and see that we are "good people"? Will we see the Perfect Son of God upon that Cross and begin to tell Him of all the wonderful things we have done? Will we merely walk by and say, "Thank you for doing that for me! I'm going to go my own way now." Only the religious heathens and loose "Christians" of the day would do as such, for they do not understand the Love and Holiness of God. They do not comprehend who they truly are and what Christ has truly done. That is why all must stand at the Cross and see Christ in the present moment of His crucifixion.

The fear of God is a fleeting reality amongst those who *profess* Christ but do not *possess* Christ. They are comfortable with how they are. They have never taken a hard, long look at the Cross; they only saw from a distance. Even if they had a chance to stand at the Cross, they viewed what Christ did only briefly. They put on their self-made veil and looked upon the Cross momentarily. They silenced and negated their senses from processing what was happening on the Cross. Quickly, they gave mental ascent that "Oh, that is nice what Jesus did. I can turn back now and return to where I came from."

This is the tragedy of self-proclaimed Christians, false converts, and counterfeit converts – they immediately turn in the other direction after viewing what Christ has done for them. Instead of desiring to get on the cross with Christ, they deny the newness of life and seek to go in their old way of living. This is the picture of those who only give mental ascent. They stand at the Cross, acknowledge Christ's actions with a condescending grin, and return to their carnality and passivity.

This is dangerous, as James warns us to "be doers of the Word, and not hearers only, deceiving yourselves" (James 1:22 ESV).

Many hear the Word. Many sit in sermons week after week, but the Word of God has no place within them. They hear It, but they do not allow It to change them. They harden at the sense of conviction. If the message is too strong, they find a pastor or church that will set their mind at ease. They seek to find those who will briefly speak on what Christ has done and those who secretly promote sin. They will go to a church that says nothing about sin. Instead, they will look for something that is like a motivational concert. The music is disruptive and does not glorify God.

Entertainment takes precedence over revering God. Messages are no longer based upon the Word and guided by the Spirit. Instead, they are worked up in the flesh. They are made with one purpose: "What will make men come to my church and keep them coming." Truth is irrelevant from these so-called churches claiming Christ but not knowing Him. The Holy Spirit's presence is not within that church, for that church trusts in the minds and machinery of men. There is no honest thirst and desire for God, only man's applause. There is no genuine desire to see souls saved, only to be externally attractive and relevant to the world.

Those who go to such churches are those who have itching ears. "For the time will come when they will not endure sound doctrine, but according to their own desires, *because* they have itching ears, they will heap up for themselves teachers; and they will turn *their* ears away from the truth, and be turned aside to fables" (2 Timothy 4:3-4 NKJV). That is exactly why Paul says earlier in Timothy 4:1-2 (NKJV), "I charge *you* therefore before God and the Lord Jesus Christ, who will judge the living and the dead at His appearing and His kingdom: Preach the word! Be ready in season *and* out of season. Convince, re-buke, exhort, with all longsuffering and teaching."

Those who arrive at the Cross but do not get on the Cross are those who are lost. For any preacher that preaches a cross without a cost is lost. Anyone who claims the way in partiality is a false prophet and must be dealt with accordingly.

As Christians, we do not judge the character of men but the doctrine they preach. If someone preaches a soft, smooth message with no conviction, we can instantly discern that message is not of God nor from God. If a church and pastor truly possessed the Holy Spirit, there would be conviction. ""Nevertheless I tell you the truth. It is to your advantage that I go away; for if I do not go away, the Helper will not come to you; but if I depart, I will send Him to you. And when He has come, He will convict the world of sin, and of right-eousness, and of judgment"" (John 16:7-8 NKJV).

Anyone can wear a cross around their neck, but few possess a cross within their heart. Anyone can claim the name of Jesus as Savior but not live as if He were Lord. Due to this, and the accelerated rate of people who claim Jesus and think they are saved, we have a generation filled with misguided "Christians". Few there be who find the Way of Christ and go in the Way. ""Because narrow *is* the gate and difficult *is* the way which leads to life, and there are few who find it"" (Matthew 7:14 NKJV).

We must see ourselves for who we are as we stand at the Cross. We must not seek to hide anything (as if we could do so before the Omnipresent Eye and Omniscient Mind of God). We must be honest and declare, "I am a sinner."

"As it is written: "There is none righteous, no, not one; There is none who understands; There is none who seeks after God. They have all turned aside; They have together become unprofitable; There is none who does good, no, not one."

"Their throat *is* an open tomb; With their tongues they have practiced deceit"; "The poison of asps *is* under their lips"; "Whose mouth *is* full of cursing and bitterness." "Their feet *are* swift to shed blood; Destruction and misery *are* in their ways; And the way of peace they have not known." "There is no fear of God before their eyes'" (Romans 3:10-18 NKJV).

We are guilty sinners before God and we must be willing to expose all we are before Christ. In doing so, all our past, sins, shame, and guilt are imparted onto Him. He takes the full blow of what we deserve.

At the Cross, we weep for our sinful past, but we also rejoice in tears for the newness of life that is to come. At the same moment, our past is forgiven, and our future is sealed. We mourn over our past but are filled with joy for the future. All this begins to happen and occur when we are honest at the Cross. If we never truly see ourselves for what we are and are honest with what we have done, we shall never truly understand what Christ did upon that Cross and comprehend the weight of our sin.

Many live as if sin weighed a few pennies on a scale, not knowing that sin weighs a few planets on top of a scale. Sin is the most wicked evil known to man because it is directly contrary to God's Word and God's Nature. Sin comes in various ways and manifests physically and mentally. Our emotions tend to hide the damage of sin. Our mental capacities seek to argue and excuse that "sin is not that bad" and "there are worse people out there."

Anyone who points the finger will never be willing to take the blame or receive rebuke. True leaders in business and sports take full responsibility for their teams and mistakes. They do not point the finger but share in the blame. So, Christ, Who is Thee Greatest Leader, has shared in our blame —

taking upon our sin while simultaneously being without sin. "For He made Him who knew no sin *to be* sin for us, that we might become the righteousness of God in Him" (2 Corinthians 5:21 NKJV).

We must be honest with ourselves and before God. We must take responsibility for the wrong we have done. If we accept that we are sinners, we can then allow the crucifixion of Christ and His Blood to cover us. This may only happen for those who see themselves for who they are as they stand at the foot of the Cross.

* * *

God of All, Who created the Heavens and the earth and loves all He has created, we humble ourselves before You. O God, You are the One Who told the waves how far they could go. You developed the laws by which we operate and are governed. You are the One in Whom all things exist. By Your Word, life is given. By Your Will, things exist. O God, how far above You are from us. Who are we, but dust amid Thy Holy Presence? God, bless us with minds that are honest with ourselves. Help us to see the Beauty of Christ upon the Cross. May we see Your Grace and Mercy at the Cross and our sin and selfishness. God, we are sinners in need of You. You are our only hope. No party, system, resources, connections, or other power can save us from our sins. It is only by the Precious Blood of Christ. O God, we repent of our sins before You. Fill us anew. Revive our weary spirits. Captivate our hearts. May we fully submit to You in all things. Take our life, and work through us for Thy glory alone. In Jesus' name, Amen.

Quotes For Meditation

1. "No one, however weak, is denied a share in the victory of the cross. No one is beyond the help of the prayer of Christ." **Pope Leo I**
2. "The more we are oppressed by the Cross, the fuller will be our spiritual joy." **John Calvin**
3. "Sin is failure to grow." **Gregory of Nyssa**
4. "The cross is not a sign of our great worth, but of our great depravity. That we were so evil that the only way we could be saved is by God's Son being crushed under the full force of the wrath that was due us." **Paul Washer**
5. "This is the crucifixion of Christ: in which He dies again and again in the individuals who were made to share the joy and freedom of His grace, and who deny Him." **Thomas Merton**

Chapter 8

Seeing Christ for Who He is

"But God demonstrates His own love toward us, in that while we were still sinners, Christ died for us." *Romans 5:8 NKJV*

Seeing the Innocent Lamb upon the Cross should bring every man and woman to their knees. How could one stand proudly at the Cross and say they need no such sacrifice? That they are "good enough" in themselves? That they can do as they please?

Who could not be moved by what Christ has done? Yet, multitudes go their own way and go astray. They turn from the image of Christ upon the Cross and live as if they have seen Him in Heaven. This image they depict is not actually Christ in Heaven, however. It is only themselves in Heaven with Christ at their side.

The thought of Heaven, not God, leads many. Their actions are not done for God but for themselves. When they view God or even think about God, they actually don't consider or think about Him at all. They think about Heaven, a byproduct of knowing and living with God forever. They think of the mansions, gold streets, and the rewards. They are carnal in every regard and see themselves in this place by which they are not destined to go if they do not repent and believe.

This is a sad reality for many. On that Final Day, Christ will tell them He never knew them because many were unwilling to look at Christ on the Cross and truly see why He was there. Anyone who takes time to meditate on why the Perfect God-man is on the Cross will quickly conclude (through Scripture) that it is because of us. We are entirely responsible for our sins and for sending Christ to the Cross. We are guilty before a Holy God.

Those who take time to see Christ for Who He is on the Cross shall turn from being lost. They will not merely admire what He has done. Instead, they will prostrate and weep over the sight of Him on the Cross and themselves standing amongst transgressors. For anyone who is not willing to get on the Cross is still of the world.

Many have not died to the things of this life. They still blend in with those who are wicked, perverse, and insincere. They are still numbered amongst the transgressors and sinners of all the ages. As Denny, one of the older brothers from my prayer group always says, "We are all on equal ground at the foot of the Cross." We all stand guilty at the foot of the Cross.

Many eyes may look up and see Christ upon the Cross. Many may even have sympathy and sincerity, but this lasts only for a while. When Christ asks, "Have you come to die?" many will turn in the other direction. For the death of self is painful, but its fruits are beautiful. Those who respond with "Yes, Lord. If You were willing to die *for* me, I shall be willing to die *with* Thee" shall receive newness of life.

The beauty of what Christ has done displays so many attributes of God. God's Wrath towards sin. God's Justice towards transgressors. God's Mercy towards sinners. God's Love towards those made in His image. At the Cross, we see not a brutal tyrant seeking to damn. Not at all. At the Cross, we see a God Who was and is willing to save. We see a God willing to do what only He could do to provide the means of salvation.

When we stand at the Cross, we see the Love of Christ displayed to the world. Naked and in shame, tortured and bruised, Christ shed tears of sorrow and love. We see His weakened state and say, "My God, forgive me, a sinner!"

When we truly see Christ for Who He is, we shall say to the Roman Guard, "Not Him! Please, take me instead." Christ shall look back and tell us, "It is finished. Repent and believe, my child."

Our desire to die with Christ does not add to what He has done. We don't earn our salvation but work out our salvation (Philippians 2:12-13). To truly enter into the faith, we must do what Christ demands. We are saved only by His Blood, but His Blood will not save us if we choose to blend in with the world. "Adulterers and adulteresses! Do you not know that friendship with the world is enmity with God? Whoever therefore wants to be a friend of the world makes himself an enemy of God" (James 4:4 NKJV). If we are to be with God we are to die with Christ, and to die with Christ, we must see the love of Christ and allow it to compel us to love Him.

True love is a mutual desire that can only occur between two beings. It is not merely done by one and neglected by the other. God's love is unconditional. He loves all to the very end. However, if we are to be covered by that Love from a salvation standpoint, if we are not merely to see Christ but have Him living within, we must be born again. This occurs through a true desire and love for God.

True love is willing to sacrifice. Christ gave us the call to love Him:

- ""If anyone comes to Me and does not hate his father and mother, wife and children, brothers and sisters, yes, and his own life also, he cannot be My disciple. And whoever does not bear his cross and come after Me cannot be My disciple."" Luke 14:26-27 NKJV
- ""If you love Me, keep My commandments."" John 14:15 NKJV
- ""Greater love has no one than this, than to lay down one's life for his friends."" John 15:13 NKJV

Love that is true, noble, and pure is undefiled. It sets God in His place and keeps Him there. It doesn't merely admire God but lives as if God is truly God.

Too many treat God, Who is Majestic and Almighty, as an equal, rather than living for Him. Too many desire to merely look up and think that a simple acknowledgment is enough. What tends to destroy us is our willingness to accept or appreciate something in the mind but fail to carry it out in action and deed. Works do not save us, nor are we talking about works. We are talking about the Spirit being active and taking over the entirety of our being.

True belief leads to true possession of the Holy Spirit. When He is lively within, we are truly born again. We are led to want to be more like Christ and imitate His walk and His life.

Those who grow closer to God, gain understanding. That understanding, if met with a pure will, will seek to follow and do what is merciful, just, upright, and pure. If we understand what Christ has truly done, then a little suffering in this life is nothing compared to what God has planned for us who follow Him and endure to the very end. "For this light momentary affliction is preparing for us an eternal weight of glory beyond all comparison, as we look not to the things that are seen but to the things that are unseen. For the things that are seen are transient, but the things that are unseen are eternal" (2 Corinthians 4:17-18 ESV).

"And He Himself is the propitiation for our sins, and not for ours only but also for the whole world" (1 John 2:2 NKJV). Christ's atoning sacrifice is universally offered to all, but not all receive what He has done. Therefore, His sacrifice only covers some. The shedding of His Blood was for all to see and come under. He offers freely, but only those willing to die to sin and self shall receive everlasting help from Him Who is Love.

Sadly, though many will see Christ upon the Cross, many will turn away. Some will mock. Some will look simply out of curiosity. They, however, will never get on the Cross. They will forever stay at a distance with knowledge about God but never come to truly know God. They are those who are "always learning and never able to come to the knowledge of the truth" (2 Timothy 3:7 NKJV).

May God forever captivate us. May seeing Christ on the Cross lead us to weeping over our sin. Let us allow His Love to guide us into all Truth. Let us truly taste and see that the Lord is Good (Psalm 34:8), for we can become more than conquerors if we are found in Christ.

God has made it easy to find Christ. However, to be found in Him takes an honest evaluation of oneself, a conscious decision, and a temporary painful death. This death, however, is the most significant death to die. To die with Christ and be resurrected into newness of life leads to the most extraordinary transformation known to man.

May the love of Christ compel us not to go along with the

world or to blend in with the world. Instead, may we die with Him and declare upon our cross, "I am a born-again Christian."

* * *

Heavenly Father, Just and Pure, we praise You for Your Love and for sending Your Son to die for our sins. O Jesus, You are worthy of worship and honor. All dominion and power belong to You. All that is Good is of You. You are the One by Whom we were spoken into existence. It is through You that we can come to know the Father and the Spirit. O Christ, give us more profound revelations of the Cross. May we look upon the Cross every hour of every day, and may our worries and fears be expelled. Holy Spirit, abolish our strivings and wants. Give us the strength to die a simple, painful death as we prepare for our ascension on the cross. For it is by Your death and resurrection that we have a promised ascension. The first is painful; the second is beautiful. O God, we thank You for all things, for You are the Maker, Creator, and Sustainer of them all. In Jesus' name, Amen.

Quotes For Meditation

1. "By the cross we know the gravity of sin and the greatness of God's love toward us." **John Chrysostom**
2. "Never did God so manifest His hatred of sin as in the death and sufferings of His only Begotten Son." **Jonathan Edwards**
3. "Not only do we not know God except through Jesus Christ; We do not even know ourselves except through Jesus Christ." **Blaise Pascal**
4. "There is no greater message, no greater thought than what Christ has done for us on the cross." **Paul Washer**
5. "Let us look upon a crucified Christ, the remedy of all our miseries. His cross hath procured a crown, His passion hath expiated our transgression. His death hath disarmed the law, His blood hath washed a believer's soul. This death is the destruction of our enemies, the spring of our

happiness, and the eternal testimony of Divine love." **Stephen Charnock**

Chapter 9

Looking Up to the Cross

"**B**ut He was wounded for our transgressions, He was bruised for our iniquities; The chastisement for our peace was upon Him, And by His stripes we are healed." Isaiah 53:5 NKJV

At the Cross, an undeserving death provided reason and hope for the world.

In Christ, all things unfold, and by Him, all things enfold. Christ is the One Who spoke everything into existence. "In the beginning was the Word, and the Word was with God, and the Word was God. He was in the beginning with God. All things were made through Him, and without Him nothing was made that was made. In Him was life, and the life was the light of men. And the light shines in the darkness, and the darkness did not comprehend it" (John 1:1-5 NKJV).

Christ is our only hope. If we are to know God, it is through Christ. If we exist, it is because we were spoken into existence by Christ, Who is the Word. The Word is the most potent

Voice known to man. By the Word, man is convicted and converted. By the Word, things are created and destroyed.

The Word is founded on Truth, Goodness, Justice, and Holiness. There is nothing that can thwart the Word. It is by the Word that what we see is as is, so long as it is. It is through the Word that God's other unique attributes are manifested and made known.

Christ alone had to die on the Cross. When we look up and see the anguish, heartbreak, and precious face of Jesus, we cannot help but remain silent. We could not have gone to the Cross as Christ did. We could not have offered up our son as a living sacrifice.

No one in the world could take on the full blow of the wrath of God due to sin—a simple act with profound implications. A message easily understood but continues to unravel greater understanding. It is the Cross of Christ we must meditate and think on.

When looking up to the Cross, we are undistracted by the cares of this life. We begin to see Him, Who is the Light, become temporal darkness. We see this Precious Lamb being slain upon the Cross. We see the God-man forsaken by His own Father.

Looking up at the Cross, we recognize how far we have fallen. For with God, we always look up in a hopeful manner that knows He is High and Lifted Up. At the same time, our spiritual disposition remains low. We prostrate before the One Who did what only He could do.

"For to this you were called, because Christ also suffered for us, leaving us an example, that you should follow His steps: "Who committed no sin, Nor was deceit found in His mouth"; Who, when He was reviled, did not revile in return; when He suffered, He did not threaten, but committed *Himself* to Him Who judges righteously; Who Himself bore our sins in His own body on the tree, that we, having died to sins, might live for righteousness—by Whose stripes you were healed. For you were like sheep going astray, but have now returned to the Shepherd and Overseer of your souls" (1 Peter 2:21-25 NKJV).

Amid every ability to accuse and destroy man, Christ resisted. He alone was Perfect and fulfilled the call of the Father. He was not filled with deceit or guilty of any wrong. The Innocent became sin. "For He made Him who knew no sin *to be* sin for us, that we might become the righteousness of God in Him" (2 Corinthians 5:21 NKJV).

As we look to the Cross and understand our wretched state, we cannot help but wonder why Christ would go to such lengths! We stand confused, humbled, and in reverence at the foot of the Cross. We see no greater love than that of Christ, Who sacrificed His life on behalf of ours, Who became sin on our behalf that we might be found righteous.

O, the blessed gift of Christ we can receive! How misguided multitudes are in trying to pervert the crucifixion of Christ to build up systems and make Christ's death a means to social reform. Many are misguided and do not know the One, True Gospel—that every man is a sinner, Christ died for man's sins, and we are called to repent of our sins and believe in Christ!

May we never succumb or allow anything else to come into the Gospel message when viewing the Cross, for it is a story of Infinite Glory.

Christ on the Cross was an all-in-one act and demonstration of that which is. Sin and evil were revealed. God's wrath and justice were known. Christ's Love and Grace were magnified. The ability to go from darkness to Light, spiritually dead to alive, damned to saved was provided.

O how God desires to save those who are lost. How could we deny or reject God? How could we want to go another way or turn aside? How could we find ourselves in no need of Christ's atoning sacrifice? Only those who are selfish, deceived, and wicked shall be amongst those who mock at the foot of the Cross.

Although man may look up and mock Christ, we choose to humble ourselves and admit that we are sinners. We choose not to be like "those who passed by" and "blasphemed Him, wagging their heads and saying, "Aha! *You* who destroy the temple and build *it* in three days, save Yourself, and come down from the cross!" Likewise, the chief priests also, mocking among themselves with the scribes, said, "He saved others; Himself He cannot save. Let the Christ, the King of Israel, descend now from the cross, that we may see and believe." Even those who were crucified with Him reviled Him" (Mark 15:29-32 NKJV).

Man is foolish. We know not what we do. We are more sinful than we realize. We are scoffers who are deceptive and guilty of many sins. How could God foreknow all this and still choose to send Christ to the Cross? May we look up at the Cross and see someone who does not seek to destroy us. May we not deceive ourselves into thinking that Christ did it all for Himself and wants us to be servants to worship Him. Though Christ deserves all the glory, and though we are called to be His servants (for it is in being a servant to Christ we are free from all else), "God demonstrates His Own love toward us, in that while we were still sinners, Christ died for us" (Romans 5:8 NKJV).

True, Biblical, everlasting Love is only found in Christ. May we look up and see Him suffering for our sake. Not because we are worth it but simply because of Who He is.

Blessed be the name of the Lord Jesus Christ, always.

* * *

Triune God, You are the Great I AM. You are above all, beyond all, in all, and through all. You sustain man by Your will and give each man unique gifts and talents. You alone, O God, made man upright. Yet, we have sought out many schemes. You alone desired to keep us from the consequences of sin. Yet, we fell astray and wanted to be as You. God, none are like You, nor will be like You. You alone Rule and Reign Supreme. You are the Alpha and Omega. You are the One Who loves us and sent Christ to the Cross. O God, may we see ourselves for who we are and see You for Who You are. May our eyes gaze upon the Cross and see the distorted figure of Christ possessing a Spirit stronger than any of us could ever have or manifest on our own. Amid the most gruesome sight, may we see the simple gaze of Christ looking back at us, calling us to repent. May we rejoice and give Him all the praise. God, help us not merely to stand, looking at the Cross, but to kneel before You in reverent awe of how You, the God of Glory, would be willing to save sinners like us. We humble ourselves before Thee, the Eternal One. In Jesus' name, Amen.

Quotes For Meditation

1. "The illusions of this world soon vanish, especially if a man arms himself with the Sign of the Cross. The devils tremble at the Sign of the Cross of our Lord, by which He triumphed over and disarmed them." **St. Anthony Abbot**

2. "The glory of God shines, indeed, in all creatures on high and below, but never more brightly than in the Cross." **John Calvin**

3. "Our greatest ambition must be to see the crucified Christ always before us, His life and death, what efforts He demands of us. Seek nothing beyond this. It will please the Divine Master. His real friends ask only for those things that will enable them to fulfill His commissions. Any other desire, any other quest, is but self-love, spiritual pride, an encirclement by the Devil." **Lorenzo Scrupoli**

4. "Whoever removes the Cross and its interpretation by the New Testament from the center, in order to replace it, for example, with the social commitment

of Jesus to the oppressed as a new center, no longer stands in continuity with the apostolic faith." **Hans Urs von Balthasar**

5. "The only cross in all of history that was turned into an altar was the cross on which Jesus Christ died. It was a Roman cross. They nailed Him on it, And God, in His majesty and mystery, turned it into an altar. The Lamb Who was dying in the mystery and wonder of God was turned into the Priest Who offered Himself. No one else was a worthy offering." **A.W. Tozer**

Chapter 10

Kneeling Before Christ

" **C**hrist *has redeemed us from the curse of the law, having become a curse for us (for it is written, "Cursed is everyone who hangs on a tree"), that the blessing of Abraham might come upon the Gentiles in Christ Jesus, that we might receive the promise of the Spirit through faith." Galatians 3:13 NKJV*

Those who stand with honesty before the Cross will kneel in all humility. They will revere God and be led to repentance. By seeing the consequences of our sin, we will be led to want to turn from our sin.

A wicked man may forever indulge in lust and sin, but those born-again will forever hate and want to drift from sin.

Anyone can stand before the Cross, but few will bend their knee to It. Not that the Cross itself is what we are to worship, but Him Who is on the Cross.

Those who never kneel in contrition before the Cross will never have a guaranteed ascension. They are lost and remain as they are if they do not humble themselves and repent, for anyone can go up to a person and say the right words. Anyone can nod their head and give mental assent. Anyone can pretend and put on a façade. The difference between the true believer and the one who puts on a show is the disposition of the heart.

Our externals reflect the heart. Eventually, what is harbored within will be seen without. Counterfeit converts rarely speak about Christ yet freely accept what He did (without truly understanding what He has done based upon God's standards). If we are to follow Him, we are to deny self. Those who believe they are saved but do not follow Him are those who do not have the Holy Spirit. Their sin does not convict them. Instead, they attempt to excuse or conceal their sin. They strive in the flesh to do everything externally that makes them appear righteous, but in their striving, they look like the Pharisees.

There is a deeper, more difficult discernment that can be found in counterfeit converts who do speak about Christ. They are willing to share what He has done. They will say, "Christ died on the Cross because He loves you." However, they will entirely drift from the message of sin and *why* Christ went to the Cross.

Many will stand for love but will not kneel in repentance over their sin. Many will stand in the pride of thinking they are saved, but few will ever take the time to kneel with a broken heart.

Honest tears always come from a posture that is broken. Kneeling before the Cross reveals to God, ourselves, and others that we do not think we have anything or are anything without Christ. When we kneel, the entire disposition of our heart is manifested to the world. This is followed not merely in an act but in our countenance. A man or woman can even kneel temporarily and be dismissed into thinking that a "one-time act of humility will save."

However, God makes it very clear that we are to die to ourselves daily (Luke 9:23). Anyone can practice a virtue and exercise it. It is one thing to portray a virtue but another to live out a virtue. Just because a good act is done does not make someone good. A man could be sentenced to prison for killing ten people. They could share their food with someone of higher status in prison, only to join that group and be part of a gang that seeks to intimidate and even kill other prisoners. Good acts do not lead to overall goodness.

Likewise, one act of humility does not determine someone's destiny. Anyone can pretend. Anyone can do something once and never again. True born-again people shall remain kneeling until Christ discerns the heart and tells us to rise. If we desire to be with Christ, we must take up our cross with Christ. We cannot rise in purity if we cannot descend in humility.

The great saints of old knew and understood this. It took a few Chapters in the Book of Job for God to absolutely dismantle and humble Job. God lovingly brought forth strong words of rebuke to Job to confront his self-righteousness. How does Job respond? ""I have heard of You by the hearing of the ear, But now my eye sees You. Therefore I abhor *myself*, And repent in dust and ashes"" (Job 42:5-6 NKJV).

Any man or woman who sees Christ upon the Cross and is destined to be born-again will initially hate themselves. They will not despise their image but their spirituality. It takes inner eyes to discern what we have not been in our metaphysical senses. Our mind, soul, and spirit have been corrupted numerous times, and we are guilty before the Holy One of Israel.

When the Spirit speaks, we are brought to nothing. We

repent in dust and ashes and desire to be raised and transformed.

Anyone who willingly looks at their inner life and takes time to reflect will see that they are guilty of much more than they initially thought. Lust, envy, pride, narcissism, lack of empathy, lack of compassion, an unwillingness to be reproved, resentment, boastfulness, money-hungry, unrelenting anger, lack of faith and depression, continued anxiousness – all these things are not from God and contrary to God. Those who kneel before the Cross accept that these are not of God and that they are guilty of them.

God, in His Grace and Mercy, lovingly speaks to us and assures us that when we go to die with Christ, these things shall die. We shall be made new and transformed. These things will no longer have dominion, and God will help us every step of the way. For "the righteous falls seven times and rises again, but the wicked stumble in times of calamity" (Proverbs 24:16 NKJV).

It is not merely in a one-time act that we are saved. It is what both lead to and will follow that past act. Only God knows the beginning from the end. "For I *am* God, and *there is* no other; I *am* God, and *there is* none like Me, Declaring the end from the beginning, And from ancient times *things* that are not *yet* done, Saying, 'My counsel shall stand, And I will do all My pleasure'" (Isaiah 46:9-10 NKJV). God is the Discerner of our minds and hearts (Jeremiah 17:10). He knows if the one-time act reflects genuineness and authenticity.

The man or woman who kneels before the Cross will be authentic in their humble disposition. The median of this act is an honest reflection of what has been and a lifelong desire to be what only can occur through Christ. If God foreknows that a person will be committed on this road and truly desires to change, they shall be saved. Again, this is not due to the instant kneeling but to the discerning of the genuineness of the kneeling and if this will be a continued occurrence—a willingness to repent when in the wrong and seek God for deliverance and strength.

Only God knows the authenticity, and time reveals all true conversions. Someone can say something about the faith and look to be on fire for God, only to backslide and leave the faith months later.

When you are a Christian long enough, you see this occur. Instant zeal for the faith does not guarantee true conversion. Anyone can be zealous about something. This is called "motivation"; if it is not balanced with discipline and control, it will eventually fade. It will not last long because it was an instant burst of excitement and motivation, only to be proven a lie as the desire fled. Motivation is instant desire and zeal, whereas lifestyle is filled with disciplines and attributes of what is needed and believed.

Anyone can be excited about building a startup. Anyone can be motivated by a great idea. If there is no long-term commitment to do what must be done, it results in nothing.

No one cares about ideas unless they are acted upon. It is the same with the faith. True faith is not merely this idea that we believe and get excited about at one time in our lives. True faith is active and leads to activity, both internally and externally. True faith is repentant faith. True faith produces the attributes of the faith, for we do not work *for* our salvation, but we do work *out* our salvation (Philippians 2:12).

We must understand that kneeling before the Cross dictates whether we will get up and choose to turn back to the way we came or if we will stand, place our cross beside Christ's, and be willingly nailed. The first merely gives temporary recognition. The latter acknowledges what has been done and what must be done further. To truly enter into what

Christ has done, we must kneel before the Cross and prepare to die.

"For by grace you have been saved through faith, and that not of yourselves; *it is* the gift of God, not of works, lest anyone should boast" (Ephesians 2:8-9 NKJV). Faith is not a temporal instance that comes and goes. We are saved solely by what Christ has done, but we cannot be saved by what He has done until we willingly accept what He has done and both believe and follow what He has declared. If we do not take up our cross, then we cannot be His disciple. ""And he who does not take his cross and follow after Me is not worthy of Me. He who finds his life will lose it, and he who loses his life for My sake will find it"" (Matthew 10:18-19 NKJV).

The walk of faith is for those who are spiritually weak, recognize their weakness, and cling to Christ as their strength.

Counterfeit converts are the opposite. They are weak in heart and believe themselves to be spiritually strong. They pride themselves in delusion and deception. They live a fantasy. They are unwilling to repent. They are weak in heart because they are unwilling to face the tough truths and reality of what lingers within them. They believe themselves to be spiritually strong by externals, and other virtues deceive them in cunning ways. Sadly, this is what leads many astray.

That is why it is only the meek who will inherit the earth. However, to be meek before God, we must be strong in following God. This is only done by the Holy Spirit. However, it takes a strong heart to know God and truly make our own independent decision.

A strong heart is found as courageous. It seeks to be honest and is strong enough to say, "I am in the wrong. I am not what I should be. I am a sinner. O God, have mercy upon me. Help me! Save me! You alone are my only Hope."

A weak heart will never follow in like manner because its

weakness comes from believing it is spiritually strong and not needing assistance or aid from God. Even if it temporarily sees the need, it will not do as Christ commands. It will be unwilling because it is weak and unwilling to be confronted when wrong.

May God give us the strength and power to kneel before the Cross of Christ. May our disposition be one of humility and honesty. Through our genuineness of wanting to become one with Christ in Spirit, we shall be saved by Christ.

It is never what is instantly or merely done that saves us. It is only by God's Grace through true faith. True faith is long-lasting. It is ongoing. It is enduring. It is persevering. It is willing to go to the lengths that God commands, knowing He is there to comfort, strengthen, and help us in times of need.

May we kneel before the Cross until we hear the words from Christ declare, "Arise, My child. Deny yourself and die with Me. In Me, you will have life more abundantly. I have seen your heart's intent and it is pure. Suffer with me awhile, and you shall receive everlasting life. Be willing to die to self and sin, and you shall receive My Spirit and become born-again."

Blessed is the man or woman who kneels at the Cross of Christ, lamenting over their sin, repenting of their sin, and preparing to die and be raised to newness of life.

* * *

Lord Jesus, You did what no other could do. You took the full blow of sin and shame. You are the One to Whom we can come before and kneel. We can repent and turn from our wicked ways. O God, thank You for the gift of salvation. Thank You that we don't have to live in our carnality. In You alone is fulfillment and newness of life. In You, God, we have a promised hope of everlasting joy and jubilation in Heaven. God, we kneel before You in humility. May our disposition remain real and authentic. May we be honest with You and ourselves. God, keep us from going wayward. Keep us from going astray. May we be obedient unto our physical death. May we be changed through our spiritual transformation. As we die to self, we trust in You to see us through to the very end. Bless us with the fear of You, we pray. In Jesus' name, Amen.

Quotes For Meditation

1. "Silence is the cross on which we must crucify our ego." **Seraphim of Sarov**
2. "The saints were people like all of us. Many of them came out of great sins, but by repentance they attained the Kingdom of Heaven. And everyone who comes there comes through repentance, which the merciful Lord has given us through His sufferings." **St. Silouan the Athonite**
3. "Jesus died on the cross to purchase peace with God for me — and He is in Heaven now to maintain that peace, for me and in me." **David Wilkerson**
4. "The cross tends high above the opinions of men and to that cross all opinions must come at last for judgment." **A.W. Tozer**
5. "It costs God nothing, so far as we know, to create nice things: but to convert rebellious wills cost Him crucifixion." **C.S. Lewis**

Part Three

Hoisting The Cross

Chapter 11

Hoisting The Cross

"Dear Lord, when looking up at Thee, I see Thy loving eyes on me, Love overflows my humble heart, Know what a faithful friend Thy art. A cup of sorrow I foresee, Which I accept for love of Thee, Thy painful way I wish to go, The only way to God I know. My soul is full of peace and light, Although in pain, this light shines bright. For here Thou keep to Thou breast. My longing heart to find there rest. Leave me here freely all alone, In cell where never sunlight shone. Should no one ever speak to me, This golden silence makes me free! For though alone, I have no fear, Never wert Thou, O Lord, so near. Sweet Jesus, please, abide with me! My deepest peace I find in Thee. Amen." Blessed Titus Brandsma (Martyred in Dachau Concentration Camp in WWII)

When it comes to hoisting the cross, the lonely journey turns into a lonely crucifixion. Though Christ is before us, we must face the harshness of being crucified upon our cross. We must be nailed on the cross with Christ to receive new life.

When a cross is hoisted, it is for all to see. Many will have different opinions and perceptions. Many will cease to understand. Many will hide their fear of the call of God through mockery and ridicule. These are mere pebbles amid our crucifixion, for we are called to die to self and live in the Spirit; and if we are to receive the Spirit, we must prepare ourselves to receive the Spirit. We must be willing to allow our lives to be on full display. Others must see that we have come to the Cross of Christ to die alongside Him.

Only those serious about the faith will be willing to see the imagery of hoisting the cross. This is a symbol to the world that we are no longer of the world. We have chosen that which is not easy to receive that which is full of glory and beauty.

Salvation can only come by way of death. When we make it evident to the world that we no longer desire to pursue that which the world gives, the world will enhance the feeling of loneliness upon us. When we choose to die, their insults will seek to make us believe we are all alone.

Though we hang upon our cross alone, we are not alone. When we are hoisted while hanging on the cross, we see Christ beside us. He is already there, waiting for us to follow in likemanner.

Christ did not deserve His crucifixion, but we are responsible for ours. We are guilty. The only way to be set free is to be covered by the Blood, and to be covered by the Blood means to have a faith that dies to self and seeks Christ for assistance in all things.

The process of hoisting our cross is a willingness to join our body to the cross, allowing the pain of being nailed to the cross to have its place, to hang before men and the world and suffer the pain and conviction that is to occur, and finally, shedding tears of both sorrow and joy.

A man who dies with Christ upon the Cross shall experience what is both painful and glorious. An all-in-one expression comes forth when our cross is hoisted. We know that the end is near, though there is still time requested of us to hang on the cross.

May God give us understanding behind the hoisting of the Cross. This is the third phase of our journey that must be understood and take place. If we are unwilling to hoist our cross, then our faith will be a shameful one kept only in private rather than a bold and courageous one that stands before the public.

May the Spirit help us to be fortified as we face our death, prepared and ready.

Chapter 12

Willingly Joining the Body to the Cross

"Then He said to them all, *"If anyone desires to come after Me, let him deny himself, and take up his cross daily, and follow Me.""* Luke 9:23 NKJV

When it comes time to hoist our cross, we must first be willing to join our body to the cross. This inner crucifixion that is to occur is painful and is one by which we can only endure through humility. In our willingness to join our inner man to the pains of the cross, we reveal that our faith shall not be awakened as soft or light. We do not see faith as this easy, ongoing process by which we are comfortable, for true faith entails difficulty.

True faith cannot be lived out unless by the Spirit. If we are willing to join our body to the cross, we reveal to the world that we would rather go through the painful process of crucifying self than exalting self and receiving damnation.

Those willing to join their body to the cross will allow the flesh to be crucified. This includes all aspects of ego, self, entitlement, complacency, and any form of the flesh you can name. The one who is willing to die to the flesh and the world is the one who goes from demanding their own rights to being ready to lay down every one of them.

No one enters the faith that is not required to leave something behind. In every born-again believer's life, we are called to die to that which is contrary to God and His nature. Whatever contradicts His Word is an abomination.

"The LORD saw that the wickedness of man was great in the earth, and that every intention of the thoughts of his heart was only evil continually" (Genesis 6:5 ESV). We know "That God made man upright, But they have sought out many schemes" (Ecclesiastes 7:29 NKJV). God originally made us perfect, and we corrupted that perfection by choosing to do what was against God.

God always declares what is, based upon Who He is. If He warns us not to go in the way of the scornful and the sinners, He says it for our protection. For every sin known to man brings forth consequence. These consequences could be immediate or prolonged. They could last a short time or ruin one's reputation for life. Whatever the case, God tells us to go in the way of the Word and to be led by His Spirit.

If we are unwilling to join our body to the Cross, we reveal that we want Jesus *and* our sin. We are reluctant to lay down all we have for Christ. We refuse to heed His Word, His correction, and reproof. This is the most dangerous form of faith. A faith that knows *about* God but does not *know* God. A faith that hears what is being demanded but chooses to deceptively think that they can live both in the world and of the world.

"And do not be conformed to this world, but be transformed by the renewing of your mind, that you may prove what *is* that good and acceptable and perfect will of God" (Romans 12:2 NKJV). We are called to higher ground. We are to be transformed, and true transformation only occurs when we are willing to be changed. When we are confronted with the guilt of our sin, we can choose to willingly join our body to the cross, and prepare to be nailed; or, as many, we can carry our cross and go no further in the process of being willing to die.

This is another scary reality. Many carry their cross for but a time. They hear the call and finally get to the Cross of Christ. When Christ commands them to not merely carry their cross to Him, but to die with Him, they lose interest.

Though the cross represents those cursed and in pain, many self-professed Christians see their cross as a need to sacrifice everything but their internal state. They make sacrifices of giving money to the poor, sacrificing hobbies and life pursuits to help others. They create their own cross while forsaking what the Cross actually represents and means. Rather than accepting the call to die to sin, they create their own cross to sacrifice to "make the world a better place."

""Has the LORD as great delight in burnt offerings and sacrifices, as in obeying the voice of the LORD? Behold, to obey is better than sacrifice, and to listen than the fat of rams"" (1 Samuel 15:22 ESV). We live in a day where we don't have to sacrifice to God when we sin. The Blood of the Perfect, Holy, atoning sacrifice of the Lord Jesus Christ can cover us. Yet, many in the crowd today choose to either neglect what Christ has done or pervert what Christ has done. This is especially prevalent among those who don't want to hear anything about crosses and losses. Instead, they create for themselves the need to continually make sacrifices to God and seek His blessing and approval by means of externals.

"God, do you not see what I have had to sacrifice? I have given my money and time to help the poor and needy. I have taken care of the widow and oppressed. Do you not see all that

I have done?" The tragedy in this is it is a *partial* fulfillment of the command of God. "Religion that is pure and undefiled before God the Father is this: to visit orphans and widows in their affliction, and to keep oneself unstained from the world" (James 1:27 ESV).

Those who go on this path claim the former but ignore the latter. They work out the external good that can benefit others but do not give up the inner corruption that crucified Christ. They love to praise themselves for how much they have sacrificed to God, neglecting the most important call that began Christ's ministry: REPENT. "From that time Jesus began to preach, saying, "Repent, for the kingdom of heaven is at hand"" (Matthew 4:17 ESV).

Not only are they unwilling to repent and keep themselves unstained by the world, but their pursuit of justifying themselves is also selfish. It excludes the reason for Christ's sacrifice. Those who fall prey to this mindset continue in the realm of self. This self is hidden, but it is still unwilling to join the body to the Cross.

Instead, it argues as if to say, "Christ, I carried my cross up to You, and You still aren't giving me the desires of my heart. You have not kept Your promises. I feel like all I have done is in vain." The tragedy is it is all in vain. It is still working in the flesh for salvation or God's approval.

Anyone who claims to work for God while neglecting to lay down sin has made themselves their own "god". They have chosen the easy, self-created path. This path boosts ego and self. It does not get rid of that which led Christ to the Cross. Rather, it bases all that they are on the externals of life and what they do.

God does not need any of us. His call for our lives is to our benefit, but it does not *aid* in His Will. His Ultimate Will shall occur whether we fulfill His call for our lives or not. His Will shall move forward, whether we obey or not. God's Will is the Unending, Unconquerable Force that accomplishes what He desires. God's Perfect Will may not be fulfilled (in the sense that He desires all to come to repentance and believe in Him (1 Timothy 2:4, 2 Peter 3:9)), but His Ultimate, Divine Will shall be completed. For God can raise up stones to do what we can do if He so desires (Matthew 3:9).

Works, therefore, are a byproduct of our faith. Works do not save us. Rather, they are a sign that we are saved. Those who claim Christ, profess to know Him, and command others to do good works while neglecting to distance themselves from the world are counterfeit converts. They may even carry their cross to Christ but will not willingly join their body to their own cross.

Anyone can do a good deed. Anyone can make sacrifices. However, God desires obedience more than sacrifice. In our obedience, we declare our love for Christ (John 14:15). Not merely in act and deed, but in the willingness to give up and exercise repentance when in the wrong.

As we lay down upon our cross, we reveal our submission to God, His Word, and His Will. We understand there is no getting back up once we lay ourselves down on the cross. The arms of the soldiers around us are ready to hold us down as we prepare to be nailed. The most painful process is yet to come, but its fruits will be bountiful.

O, the beauty of one unwilling to back away from God's tougher call and Truths! How blessed is the one who reveals his submission to God by laying down his life for the sake of receiving newness of life!

The wood shall pain our back. The blisters that enter our skin are the initial pains of conviction. This conviction is what will have us begin the process of crying out to God, "Forgive me, a sinner."

Blessed is the one who not only goes to the Cross and arrives at the Cross — blessed is the one who takes their cross and willingly spreads themselves upon it, not in fear, but in the assurance that we are following Christ's way to receive what He can give by being crucified with Him.

* * *

Blessed Savior, Who is Lord and Ruler of all, we submit ourselves before Thee. God, come now and build in us the courage and confidence to lay down our lives before You. You do not need us, but You command us to die. O, to be slain with Christ is a beautiful gift! To know that a coming spiritual resurrection and bodily ascension is on its way is a great promise. God, we join ourselves to the pain of our cross. You have appointed it to us. As we prepare to be nailed, may our inner life continually surrender all to You. May we find ourselves unworthy before You. Amid our humble contrition, may You ignite the soul's furnace with Power from On High. We seek Thee, O Holy Ghost. Bless us with the Flame of Holiness and the Kindle of Humility. We forsake the world and turn to You, the Author and Finisher of our faith. In Jesus' name, Amen.

Quotes For Meditation

1. "I am ready to die for my Lord, that in my blood the Church may obtain liberty and peace." **Thomas Becket**

2. "We give glory to You, Lord, who raised up Your Cross to span the jaws of death like a bridge by which souls might pass from the region of the dead to the land of the living... You are incontestably alive. Your murderers sowed Your living body in the earth as farmers sow grain but it sprang up and yielded an abundant harvest of men raised from the dead." **St. Ephrem the Syrian**

3. "Ye seek peace from the world; real peace is in Christ. Say not, 'peace, peace', but, 'the cross, the cross'." **Martin Luther**

4. "Woe to me if I should prove myself but a halfhearted soldier in the service of my thorn-crowned Captain." **Fidelis of Sigmaringen**

5. "The one true way of dying to self is the way of

patience, meekness, humility, and resignation to God." **Andrew Murray**

Chapter 13

Nailed to the Cross

"*And being found in appearance as a man, He humbled Himself and became obedient to the point of death, even the death of the cross.*" *Philippians 2:8 NKJV*

When a person is nailed to the cross, their gaze is upward and toward the Heavens. Amid agony, they find great joy in looking up, for they know their redemption is near. They can see the Heavens open. Just as Stephen saw the Son of Man when being stoned to death (Acts 7:54-56), so too can we see the Spirit ready to descend upon us as a dove.

When we prepare to lay down all, we shall arise with greater power and authority. Not to harm but to be the living testimony of the Power that transforms. God Almighty's Spirit is ready and prepared to enter, but first, we must be nailed and hoisted upon the Cross.

The thoughts of one laying upon the cross are varied, but

all are of the same mindset: "This must be accomplished if I am to receive that which I believe." No man or woman gained the Spirit who refused to be nailed to the cross. No man or woman who lived a life worth living remained nailed on the cross. Those who live a life worthy of the call are nailed to the cross, knowing that a coming descension from the cross and resurrection into newness of life will occur. The flesh shall die, but the spirit of man shall live. The sensuality of self can no longer be entertained when we gain spiritual eyes. These can only come from the illuminating Light and Beautified Touch of the Holy Ghost.

No one on the cross fantasizes or desires to be filled with the lusts of the flesh. They are concerned with the pain of dying. Their thoughts are, "How much more must I bear? How much longer must I be upon this cross?" Those nailed to the cross know what will come. Those destined to be holy need no one to hold them down. They need no one to force them to spread themselves upon the cross. Those who are destined to be righteous do so by their free will. They willingly lay down and prepare to be nailed.

That is the difference between the future of those destined to be godly and those who shall remain ungodly. Both have lived lifestyles of sin. The difference between the godly and ungodly is that the godly prepare to be nailed without complaining. They recognize they are guilty, and they, in the process of identifying their guilt, come willing to die. They see that the nails must pierce their flesh if they are to be a true representative of Christ.

To be hoisted before mankind on a cross makes a declarative statement: "I am guilty and I am not going back. What you see before you is the life I have chosen. I heeded the call. I came to die. I am destined to live. I am chosen by God."

The ungodly who go to the cross are forced to go. They

need guards to force them down the way to the cross. They complain and do not want to die on the cross. They are too busy with the thoughts and cares of this life. They want to go back.

Those who are spiritual criminals and want nothing to do with God, their end shall be to die on the cross. They shall die by the hand of the world. They shall go unwillingly. They shall cry and wail. They shall fear leaving this life. Their death on a cross is not the cross of Christ. Rather, it is the cross of the one who mocked Christ. It is the death of a dying man destined for damnation in Hell. It is the death of one who lived for themselves in this life and shall receive an eternity to live alone in the afterlife.

We must understand the difference between a metaphysical and physical death on the cross. Anyone can die, but not all live. So long as the Lord tarries, everyone shall die at some point, physically. ""It is the Spirit Who gives life; the flesh profits nothing"" (John 6:63 NKJV). The flesh profits nothing. When one strives for salvation in the flesh, it is vanity. Doing much in the flesh and living for self serves no merit.

To receive the Spirit, we must die. This death must be metaphysical in nature. If we do not die to self and forsake submitting and surrendering our will to God, we shall not go to the cross willingly. We shall live a lie by pretending to be nailed to the cross.

For anyone can be forced to be nailed upon a cross. However, those who will soon become children of God go willingly. They do not need others to do that which only they themselves can do. For anyone forced to go to the cross and be nailed to the cross is not genuine or authentic. They have not chosen the road less traveled. They have been too much in love with comfort and ease.

Eventually, the grip of that which has consumed them will

force them to a death they do not desire. This death will be physical; like the mocker, they will die alone in their sin. Refusing to look at Christ upon the Cross, they only see themselves and want to escape the pain they have stored up from their sin.

A spiritual man prepared to die with Christ lays down upon his cross, not in fear, but in confidence. He willingly allows himself to be nailed on the cross by God, for those who persecute the man who desires to live for God know not what they do, just as those who crucified Christ knew not what they did.

Tears are shed, not out of pain, but deep sorrow for the path the persecutors are heading if they do not repent. Those nailed to the cross hear the cheers from the godless crowd. They weep for those who do not understand that the path to life is by a willing death. Those who strive to live for this life, are heading toward an eternal death. This death is not merely a transition or an end. It is a continuation. It is an endurance in the Lake of Fire with God-given vessels who rejected the free gift of salvation and Christ's atoning sacrifice.

This sad reality comes from those not in line to be nailed to their cross. Instead, they mock from a distance. Again, even those who will be nailed to their cross by force and die to our left and right will not go willingly. They squeal and squirm. They are unwilling to repent. By neglecting to go willingly and repent, they die alone without the promise of the descension of the Holy Spirit.

This distinction must be understood. For many believe themselves to be martyrs.

Many men deem themselves as having sacrificed much. Many say they have been nailed to the cross by the hardship of the world, circumstances, government, environment, and upbringing. They are those who blame externals and do not blame themselves.

This is the difference between a weak hypocrite who hangs from a cross mocking Christ and a humble sinner preparing for change. The humble sinner goes willingly to die. The weak hypocrite goes blaming others. The humble sinner patiently and quietly spreads himself upon the cross. The weak hypocrite goes crying and walling. The humble sinner cries for those who continue to mock. The weak hypocrite cries for himself. The humble sinner claims that he is guilty before God. The weak hypocrite claims that he is guiltless and he is the way he is, due to externals. The humble sinner is ready to be changed. The weak hypocrite desires to remain the same.

"And He, bearing His cross, went out to a place called *the Place* of a Skull, which is called in Hebrew, Golgotha, where they crucified Him, and two others with Him, one on either side, and Jesus in the center. Now Pilate wrote a title and put *it* on the cross. And the writing was: JESUS OF NAZARETH, THE KING OF THE JEWS" (John 19:17-19 NKJV). The world will mock those who shall be truly born-again. They shall misrepresent us. They shall seek to defame us. They will give us all sorts of names and present false accusations. We will be misunderstood from all sides. However, we know that we are to die quietly.

We are called to suffer for the sake of Christ. The world will not understand the reality of what is taking place. By their rebellious natures, they cease to see what is happening before their eyes. Instead of acknowledging the Cross of Christ, they choose to deceive themselves. They love darkness rather than Light. Their hearts are hardened, and they do not want to hear that they are sinners. They do not want to hear God's call to come and die. Instead, they remain as they are, where they are, for the remainder of their time on Earth.

They choose to mock Christ and Who He declared Himself to be. Rather than believing in Him, they remain in their sin. They are entertained by the corruption that is within them. They continue to heap upon themselves sin upon sin.

It is amazing that despite this, Christ prays to the Father that He would forgive them. He loves all people, even when they falsely accuse Him and ridicule Him. This is love that transcends reasoning. This is love that can only come from God. In our fleshly nature, we would want to smite the mockers and prove them wrong. Christ, instead, chose to pray for them. He chose higher ground because He is the Holy One from On High. He endured the persecution and suffered for our sake. Why? Because of love.

The only thought of a man carrying a cross is death. Death of self. It is by way of death that we find Life. It is through suffering that glory is revealed. By endurance, even amid darkened anxiety and debilitating fear, we walk in the way of Christ and receive the inheritance of His death. By His death, we live. We live in this life to die - dying to self, taking up our cross, and being nailed upon the Cross with Christ.

Through our willingness to die, God is the One Who holds the Hammer of Truth. He is the One Who shall nail us to the cross. The world may perceive us being nailed and our physical death, but our metaphysical death occurs from God crucifying us. He is the One Who comforts us during our death. Simultaneously, He nails us to our cross and strengthens us to endure what is to come.

May we forever be grateful for the gift of salvation that is offered to us. May we understand that it is by our willingness to be nailed that we shall truly reveal to all others that we are destined to be new creatures as we take the faith seriously and do what the Word demands of us.

Is it painful? Yes. Is it unenjoyable at times? Absolutely. Amid these temporal feelings, however, there is Truth. There is blessing and assistance that is to come. We shall have a hope of eternal life and newness of life here on earth!

As we are nailed to the cross, we bleed from the nails entering our wrists and feet, knowing that the world is slowly oozing out of us. That which has darkened our blood is now being drained. In this process, there is spiritual blood entering us. The more of the world that comes out, the more Christ comes in.

All of this is painful and convicting, but our gaze is upward. We are not looking at the crowd or the world. We see the Heavens opening and prepare to be lifted into newness of life. We are equipping ourselves to declare, "I have been crucified with Christ; it is no longer I who live, but Christ lives in me; and the *life* which I now live in the flesh I live by faith in the Son of God, who loved me and gave Himself for me" (Galatians 2:20 NKJV).

Let us forever be focused on what is to come through our death. Let us forever look towards eternity and understand that preparing to be hung on a cross shall not last forever. One day, all things will be made new. One day, we shall be in Paradise.

May the nails sink deep so that the blood of this world pour out rapidly. For the sooner we die, the quicker we shall live.

* * *

O God of Salvation, Who is Sweet and Worthy, Who calls all to Him that they might be saved, nail us to the cross. May we no longer live for ourselves but die with Christ. May we be raised to newness of life. O God, may Your holy nails pierce our flesh. May we endure the pain of what has been, what is, and what is to come. May we suffer for Your sake. May we pray for our enemies. May we desire that all would see You through us. O God, draw us near to Thee. Focus our minds and eyes on things above. May we not give way to this life or be drawn into temptation. Deliver us from evil. Forgive us of our sins. God On High, keep us steadfast in You, we pray. In Jesus' name, Amen.

Quotes For Meditation

1. "I was no longer the center of my life and therefore I could see God in everything." **Venerable Bede**

2. "A cross without a Christ never did any man good." **John Flavel**

3. "Prostrate, see Thy cross I grasp, And Thy pierced feet I clasp; Gracious Jesus, spurn me not; On me, with compassion fraught, Let Thy glances fall. Thy cross of agony, My Beloved, look on me; Turn me wholly unto Thee; 'Be thou whole,' say openly: 'I forgive thee all.'" **Bernard of Clairvaux**

4. "The Cross, is wood which lifts us up and makes us great... The Cross uprooted us from the depths of evil and elevated us to the summit of virtue." **John Chrysostom**

5. "The old cross slew men; the new cross entertains them. The old cross condemned; the new cross amuses. The old cross destroyed confidence in the flesh; the new cross encourages it." **A.W. Tozer**

Chapter 14

Pain & Conviction

"If you endure chastening, God deals with you as with sons; for what son is there whom a father does not chasten?" Hebrews 12:7 NKJV

The chastening of the Lord humbles man and gives him an understanding that he is not as good as he thinks. Today, when everything is about boosting ego and inflating pride, chastening must take place. For without chastening, there is no true, long-lasting faith.

A faith that is real is a faith that grows over time. How do we grow? Through the conviction of the Holy Spirit. Why does conviction occur? When we are in the wrong.

If we are going to be hoisted upon the cross, then we will go through much pain and conviction. As we are hoisted up, the pain from the nails in our wrists and feet will seem unbearable. The conviction that we receive when hoisted is one that we must endure. We have come this far, and we are willing to go further for the sake of salvation. This pain we are to feel is the pain of the death of self.

As this occurs, spiritual power will soon enter, but first, the world must ooze out. As we are hoisted upon the cross, we desire to reveal to all that we are serious about our faith. For a man on a cross is a spectacle to the world that he will soon die. If it is for the purposes of faith, multitudes will see the steadfastness of our pursuit of God and willingness to surrender all to Him.

Any man who gets nailed to the cross will feel pain. From a spiritual perspective, our pain is conviction. There is nothing like conviction in this life. We feel uncomfortable when the Holy Spirit reveals that we are sinful, wicked transgressors. What we used to do without a second thought now becomes problematic to our conscience. We begin to question all we have done and finally realize that our actions have not been for God. We have not wanted to go in His way. We have desired rebellion and sin over Him Who is willing to save us and offer us that which cannot even be put into words. For the blessings of God far exceed the excitement of this world. Yet, to receive these blessings, we must not only be convicted but heed God's conviction.

Conviction leads us to the Cross. Shame keeps us from going to the Cross. When a man is convicted, he has a choice. He can choose to allow that conviction to lead him to the only place he can go to receive forgiveness and deliverance. He can choose to allow conviction to propel him forward or he can allow shame to set in.

Shame is a poor response to conviction. Shame is self-pity and indirectly exalts us above God. Anyone who suffers from shame sees themselves as too far gone from going before God. They see their sin as greater than God's Grace. This is a misguided view, and it has damaging effects. Conviction will always be from God. Shame will always be from the Enemy.

There are only four voices in this world. There is the voice of God, the Enemy, the voice of others, and our own. We can tune out the voices of others, but it can be much more challenging to tune out the voice of God and the Enemy.

God's Voice will always convict us of wrong. We cannot argue against that which He has revealed and presented.

On the other hand, we can listen to the voice of the Enemy. When we allow the Enemy to speak lies to us, we give him ground into deceiving us into thinking that we are too far gone, that we have messed up too many times, and that our past is too great for God to forgive. We become our worst enemy when we give into the Enemy's lies. Rather than coming "boldly to the throne of grace, that we may obtain mercy and find grace to help in time of need" (Hebrews 4:16 NKJV), we run further from God. We sit in self-pity.

Whether we are currently born-again or not, this can be difficult to overcome. The Enemy wants nothing to do with us knowing God. He will do anything to keep us from the desired fellowship God wants with those He created.

We know that the Enemy has come to steal, kill, and destroy (John 10:10). We know that Satan "does not stand in the truth, because there is no truth in him. When he speaks a lie, he speaks from his own *resources,* for he is a liar and the father of it" (John 8:44 NKJV). Satan will continually seek to advance his ranks by destroying our ability to come to know God. Greater still, he will implant in our minds the thoughts that would prevent us from going to God.

This is where we must understand that the Holy Spirit is for us. If we are to die to self, it doesn't matter how painful or convicting it may be; we must go. We must go in faith and by faith.

We know that we have nothing to offer God. We know there is nothing to give Him that He does not possess. All we can do is surrender our will before Him and allow Him to rule and reign in our lives. This is to our benefit, as He does not merely desire to save but to protect and bless us. These come in the ways which He knows are best. God will prove Himself faithful if we go in child-like faith, ready to die and be nailed to our cross.

Though God shall do the nailing for us to die to self on the cross, there is another cross. It is in the same cross but involves those who despise and hate us. They crucify us. They seek to destroy our reputation, deflate our image, annihilate relationships, and prevent anything good from occurring in our lives. They are not for us, but they are against us.

When we go to the cross and are crucified to the world, the world is the one who persecutes us. "For what credit *is it* if, when you are beaten for your faults, you take it patiently? But when you do good and suffer, if you take it patiently, this *is* commendable before God" (1 Peter 2:20 NKJV).

Dying to self is a good thing. If we patiently endure this process, the joy and peace that will come through this is beyond what we could fully understand, for it profits a man nothing to suffer for doing wrong. In suffering for doing right, however, there is an eternal reward.

The one who willingly faces the pain of being crucified and heeding the chastening and conviction of God shall receive a great reward. They shall not be in the wrong since they recognize that they are already in the wrong before God.

In our desire to know God and our willingness to serve Him, we begin by accepting the Greatest Sacrifice, the Lord Jesus Christ. In doing so, we become a living sacrifice. By dying to self and sin and accepting Christ, we are given the opportunity to "present (our) bodies as a living sacrifice, holy and acceptable to God, which is (our) spiritual worship" (Romans 12:1 ESV).

We must hear Christ's words and understand that "whoever does not bear his cross and come after Me cannot be My disciple" (Luke 14:27 NKJV). Only those willing to endure the pain of dying to self and responding to the conviction of the Holy Spirit about their sin shall be raised into new life. Whatever our past, whatever the hurt, suffering, sin, wickedness, cruelty, and abominations we were a part of, God can heal, deliver, redeem, and restore.

We must never place our darkness above His Light. One candle of God's Light can shine through any amount of darkness. We must be willing to listen to the reproof and instruction of God. It will be uncomfortable, but only for a season. Eventually, the Spirit of Love shall come to reside within us. We shall feel the blessed joy and peace of knowing God and possessing His Spirit.

Let us never cower at the thought of the cross. Let us face it with courage and boldness.

May we endure what is to come from God and man. For God's conviction is to lead us to salvation and Him. Man's persecution will prove whether we shall go all the way with God or abort halfway. For when trying times come, that is the testing ground of whether we truly will trust Him Who created all things. It is the ground by which we prove whether or not we are a true disciple of Christ.

Let the world test us. Let God change us. Let us forever be "rejoicing in hope, patient in tribulation, continuing steadfastly in prayer" (Romans 12:12 NKJV).

* * *

Ancient of Days, Ruler of Life, You are Him Who no man can surpass or conquer. You are Him Who convicts in love and is the God of Truth. There is no darkness in You. There is no deception within Your nature. You are Good, Holy, Pure, and Just. O God, give us the strength to endure the cross's pain and the Holy Spirit's conviction. May we not cower at the thought of death. Instead, may we gain wisdom by meditating on death. Bless us, O God of Mercy, with a deeper understanding of Your willingness to save all. You are the God of Grace and Love. You desire that none should perish but all would come to repentance. May we die to ourselves, O God, that we may be alive in the Spirit. Draw out what is not of You that lingers within us. Change us for our benefit and Your glory. Prepare us for the journey ahead, O Mighty God. In Jesus' name, Amen.

Quotes For Meditation

1. "My Lord Jesus Christ, for my sake, did wear a crown of thorns; why should not I then, for His sake, again wear this light crown, be it ever so ignominious?" **John Foxe**
2. "The way to Heaven is ascending; we must be content to travel uphill, though it be hard and tiresome, and contrary to the natural bias of our flesh." **Jonathan Edwards**
3. "Worry is the cross which we make for ourselves by over anxiety." **Francois Fenelon**
4. "Let us therefore become imitators of His endurance; and if we should suffer for His name's sake, let us glorify Him. For He gave this example to us in His own person, and we believed this." **Polycarp**
5. "We must do something about the cross, and one of two things only we can do — flee it or die upon it." **A.W. Tozer**

Chapter 15

Tears of Sorrow & Joy

"*"T*hese things I have spoken to you, that in Me you may have peace. In the world you will have tribu-lation; but be of good cheer, I have overcome the world.*"" John 16:33 NKJV*

The man hoisted on the cross has no friends. They are entirely abandoned by those who once loved them and those who currently love them the most.

Even though Mary was there to the end of her Son's death, Christ had to die alone. Not alone physically but spiritually.

Christ's Own Father forsook Him. There was no one to comfort Him. There was no one to give Him a different way. Christ had to die if we were to be offered newness of life. The joy to come first had to be met with sorrow and pain.

When hoisted upon our cross, we die to all our rights. There is no escape. Once we are nailed to the cross, we shall be hoisted for the world to see. They shall see the pain and agony of what we have endured and what we are to continue to endure.

We ourselves will begin to shed tears of both sorrow and joy. The joy of what is to come and the sorrow of the pain of conviction and what we are to endure. Our sorrow will not be one of desiring to return to our old ways. The sorrowful tears will flow because we are experiencing what Christ went through upon His Cross for our sake. We are beginning to understand the pains of what He went through because of us.

As we reflect on our lives, we see the time squandered, opportunities wasted, pursuits that led nowhere and unprofitable lifestyles. We reflect and cry the tears of regret, guilt, and shame. These tears, however, are the beginning of tears of joy. For just as quickly as we cry about what we have not been and done, we shall cry tears of thankfulness for what God has both done and will continue to do.

As the world sees these tears fall from our faces, they are witnessing the beginning of a changed and transformed lifestyle. The world will see the tears of those who are being renewed and restored. They will know that we no longer cry for the same things. We no longer shed tears for self. Instead, our tears are turned outward. They are tears of gratitude for what Christ has done and appreciation for the Father. They are tears that are preparing the heart to receive the Holy Spirit.

This is the difference between those who shed tears standing at the cross and those who shed tears while being hoisted upon the cross. The tears of those on ground level see Christ and are sorrowful over what *He* had to do, but they are not sorrowful for what *they* continue to do. They remain as they are, unchanged and unmoved. They neglect the call to come and die.

Their tears are filled with momentary, emotional bursts. There is no sorrow or remorse over what they have done in the sight of a Holy God. Their tears are shed by focusing on Christ but not following or drawing near to Him. They see what He has done and are saddened by how He is being treated. Little do those who remain on ground level know that they are the ones who are treating Him as such. Unwilling to bend or yield, they continue, sinking in their depravity. They are hardened to the reality that to truly live means we must die.

"For the wages of sin *is* death, but the gift of God *is* eternal life in Christ Jesus our Lord" (Romans 6:23 NKJV). All spiritual gifts demand sacrifice. Our sacrifice, regarding salvation, is not a working for our salvation but a working out. Our sacrifice is a demand to actively deny and die to self.

When we submit our will before God, we are prepared to receive the gift of salvation. Again, we do nothing to earn our salvation, but there is an active response to receive what God has so graciously offered. A man can offer another man a gift, but unless that man extends his arms to receive and open the gift, the gift remains unopened. It sits in the box and will not be opened to its receiver. So too, is it with the free gift of salvation and our will towards God. God has freely given us the gift of salvation, but we must actively utilize our will to reach out and take hold of what He is giving.

"For we were saved in this hope, but hope that is seen is not hope; for why does one still hope for what he sees? But if we hope for what we do not see, we eagerly wait for *it* with perseverance" (Romans 8:24-25 NKJV). A man on the cross who has come to die hopes for that which he cannot see. He does not sit and remain on the cross, hoping to get down. The man who has chosen to be crucified with Christ sets his hope on things to come and things above. His mind is engaged not with the thought of wanting to get out of his situation but rather with the desire to endure it for the sake of Christ.

Those who are strong in the faith chose the road that leads

to everlasting life through the guidance and drawing of the Holy Spirit. They go to the cross, deliberately and consciously. They were not forced to die, for they chose to die by way of the cross.

In doing so, one is hoisted for all to see. The tears that flow are filled with all emotions.

There is beauty in showing the world what one is guilty of as one neglects to conceal anything. Naked and exposed they are upon the cross. They reveal to all that they are deserving of this. They show that they have chosen this painful process and are willing to take the path of the born-again believer seriously. For no Christian ever became a Christian without the cross.

The Cross is the Symbol, Power, and Glory of God displayed to man. Not the cross in and of itself, but the act of what occurred by the Son upon the Cross. There is no greater display of Love and Justice than upon the Cross, for it is the only way by which men might be saved. Few there be who find it because few are willing to endure it.

"Do you not know that those who run in a race all run, but one receives the prize? Run in such a way that you may obtain *it*" (1 Corinthians 9:24 NKJV). We are called to finish that which we start. When we are hoisted upon the cross, there is nowhere to go. There is no choosing to get back down. No request will get us off the cross, for those who go to the cross and are nailed must die. Their death must occur before they are brought down, for a man was never crucified upon a cross that was later revealed as innocent (aside from the God-man). Those on the cross are spectacles to the world that they were in the wrong.

When we are hoisted upon the cross, the whole world sees us and rejoices. They are not happy about the transformation that is to occur. Instead, due to their iniquity and depraved states, they love to see us die. They want nothing more than for those on the path of Christ to be dead. They will mock us as we have chosen higher ground. They will clap their hands and rejoice. They will think that our chosen path will provide all sorts of restrictions. They do not understand that the cross is the path to freedom. Anyone willing to die from being a slave to sin shall be raised into newness of life and live in freedom.

Although our hoisting is a painful ascend, we shall have a beautified and sanctified ascend from death to life. The old passes away and begins to die. The blood poured out of our wrists and feet is slowly drained. The world and the things of this life are slowly oozing from us. We are no longer bound by that which used to rule us. Rather, we are hoisted above the things of this world. We are raised in the spiritual life.

The Truth of Christ compels us to endure the painful death we have yet to fully experience. Though the hoisting is just the beginning, our hope of what is to come is our promised ending.

Therefore, we cry tears of sorrow and joy. Not in wanting to go back and miss the things of the world but because we recognize the foolishness and wickedness of the world. We are not joyful to be seen by others and mocked and scoffed. Rather, we shed tears of joy because we know that "Christ is risen from the dead, *and* has become the firstfruits of those who have fallen asleep. For since by man *came* death, by Man also *came* the resurrection of the dead. For as in Adam all die, even so in Christ all shall be made alive" (1 Corinthians 15:20-22 NKJV). We have hope, joy, peace, and a great promise because of Christ.

May God strengthen us to endure what is to come. For although tears will be shed as we are hoisted upon the cross, we soon shall see the entirety of what once was and what is to be. Our death on the cross will not be sudden, but it will be extraordinary. Growth is to occur. Pain will be felt, but in the end, we shall be made as righteous, holy, purified vessels.

* * *

God in Heaven, Who provided the way of salvation, give us the courage and strength to endure the cross. Give us wisdom and understanding to look at what is to come and not what is being given up. Help us to know that what is to come by way of death will be infinitely more than what we could acquire in this life. For what does it profit a man if he gains the whole world and loses his soul? O God, what can man give in exchange for his soul? Truly, it is only the Blood of Christ that saves. May we obtain Your guidance and counsel. Be with us during our death. Do not forsake us, but empower us to fulfill the call You have for us. God, we forsake the world and turn to You, the Author and Finisher of our faith. In Jesus' name, Amen.

Quotes For Meditation

1. "Christianity has always insisted that the cross we bear always precedes the crown we wear." **Martin Luther King Jr.**

2. "The Christian life is lived in the shadow of the cross and the light of the resurrection." **John Calvin**

3. "Participation in the blessings of the union with Christ comes when the faithful have all the things needed to live well and blessedly to God." **William Ames**

4. "Christianity demands the crucifixion of the intellect." **Soren Kierkegaard**

5. "You cannot be Christ's servant if you are not willing to follow Him, cross and all. What do you crave? A crown? Then it must be a crown of thorns if you are to be like Him. Do you want to be lifted up? So you shall, but it will be upon a cross." **Charles Spurgeon**

Part Four

On The Cross

Chapter 16

On The Cross

"Let us then learn from the Cross of Jesus our proper way of living. Should I say 'living' or, instead, 'dying'? Rather, both living and dying. Dying to the world, living for God. Dying to vices and living by the virtues. Dying to the flesh, but living in the spirit. Thus in the Cross of Christ, there is death and in the Cross of Christ there is life. The death of death is there and the life of life. The death of sins is there and the life of the virtues. The death of the flesh is there and the life of the spirit." St. Aelred of Rievaulx*

As one is raised upon the cross, reality sets in. The faces, habits, and lifestyles of the ungodly become evident.

We see the futility of remaining on earth as a spiritually dead vessel. Instead, we place ourselves on the cross not out of blind submission but because we have first recognized and understood that Christ is the Way, the Truth, and the Life.

We must be willing to follow our Lord and Savior by the

Way He has paved if we desire to live in the newness and fullness of life.

When we see Christ on the Cross, we are moved in either of two directions; though, a third occurs but profits nothing. We either move away from the Cross because we deem ourselves as not needing Christ, or we move towards the Cross and prepare to get on the cross, seeing ourselves as needing to die.

The third is a lukewarm state, where recognition is had, but action and movement towards what God calls us to remain undone. In this saddened state, the mind believes, but the body is frozen. The body is unwilling to face the difficult call to die initially to obtain new life. The un-comfortability of the call to give up pleasure and the world remains an idol. The lukewarm will believe but will not move within that belief.

The Cross of Christ is monumental. Not only in what occurred but in what it calls us both to and away from. Only those with humility and courage shall know we will not remain on the cross, though we must die upon it. We will not hang there forever, though there will be a time of dying to self and being raised in the power of the Holy Spirit.

The excitement and blessedness of what is to come first begins with recognizing what Christ did upon the Cross. Once this is truly understood, one will desire to take themselves up to the hill to be crucified on their own cross.

Our cross sits behind Christ's Cross, for we can do nothing without Him. In the shadow of His Cross, we are crucified. As we are nailed to our own cross, death will soon follow. We have almost come to the point of being born-again. This painful process of hanging on the cross before men, dying to self and sin, taking the full blow of being despised and rejected, and dying on the cross with Christ will lead towards that which could not otherwise be obtained or worked up in the flesh.

As the great martyr of the faith, Justin Martyr, once said,

"You can kill us, but you cannot do us any real harm." The world, relatives, friends, and the Enemy may attempt to kill us. They may even be permitted to kill us – to crush our spirits, invade our emotions, disturb our mental fortitude, and bring forth a literal, physical death. However, whatever is to occur, the Lord is the One Who possesses our spirit and holds our soul within the palm of His Hand.

""And do not fear those who kill the body but cannot kill the soul. Rather fear Him Who can destroy both soul and body in hell"" (Matthew 10:26-28 ESV). Man can do nothing to us but what only God permits. Greater still, our spiritual senses and metaphysical nature belongs solely to God. No one can do anything permanently regarding the incorporeal aspect of our nature.

Therefore, when we die on the cross, we may die by way of other men. If we go willingly, however, we shall see them as aiding in the death of our ego, pride, way, and self. They will be those who may crush us and even seek to destroy us. However, if we go willingly, real harm will not be done. For "to live is Christ, and to die is gain" (Philippians 1:21 ESV).

Chapter 17

Hanging on the Cross Before Men

T hen they will deliver you up to tribulation and kill you, and you will be hated by all nations for My name's sake."" Matthew 24:9 NKJV

A man who hangs from a cross is a public display of humiliation.

Whether that man is falsely accused or rightfully crucified, they cannot escape the despise and ridicule from those who currently go unpunished. For Christ, He was Perfect and wrongly crucified. For us, we are sinners and deserving of the disgrace from the world. ""If you were of the world, the world would love its own. Yet because you are not of the world, but I chose you out of the world, therefore the world hates you""" (John 15:19 NKJV). This hatred is displayed in many forms but becomes most prevalent when we are about to make the greatest transition.

Though John 15:19 pertains to those born-again, we experience the same hatred from the world just as we are about to become born-again. They hate that we are thinking about the deeper truths of life. They hate that we have the strength to admit we are in the wrong. They hate that we are willing to take responsibility for our misconduct and sin. They hate that we are about to move into the Light and are willing to be exposed.

Any soon-to-be-born-again Christian hanging on the cross with Christ will be despised. They will receive names, backlash, and opposition. Even those closest to them will attempt to manipulate them into staying in their old ways.

Naturally, the heart of man desires that others would remain where they are so that they themselves can remain where they are. No one naturally likes change. It takes growth and a willingness to go beyond mediocrity. We all have this within us, but not all have the perseverance and grit to follow through.

As we have chosen to go to the Cross and hang on our cross, we will hear the words of those still caught in their iniquity. We will be entirely stripped of all we have ever done, all we have ever known.

The man known for his humor will go through a transition of forsaking sexual, inappropriate jokes. The man who was the life of the party will refrain from going to parties. The one everyone wanted to hook up and sleep with will deny the fulfillment of wanting to date for the sake of one-night stands.

A significant death is occurring and taking place — one that people cannot deny but will mock to the very end. That is why those who willingly hang upon a cross before men are those who do so without remorse and complaining. They do not cry from the tree on which they are nailed. They do not demand the public to get them down. Instead, they hang upon the cross, willingly taking in the full blow of conviction from God and the mockery of men as they transition from death to life. For they heard the still small voice of the Holy Spirit say, "This is the way, walk in it" (Isaiah 30:21). They hold onto the hope of what is to come and are willing to endure this painful death into an empowered life.

"Beloved, do not think it strange concerning the fiery trial which is to try you, as though some strange thing happened to you; but rejoice to the extent that you partake of Christ's sufferings, that when His glory is revealed, you may also be glad with exceeding joy. If you are reproached for the name of Christ, blessed *are you,* for the Spirit of glory and of God rests upon you. On their part He is blasphemed, but on your part He is glorified. But let none of you suffer as a murderer, a thief, an evildoer, or as a busybody in other people's matters. Yet if *anyone suffers* as a Christian, let him not be ashamed, but let him glorify God in this matter" (1 Peter 4:12-16 NKJV).

Every born-again believer will experience suffering in their transition phase from death to life and through the remainder of their life. No man ever came to the cross without first being convicted of why they must come. God must first reveal the cancer within all of us if we are to receive His healing touch. That is why the man who hangs willingly on the cross differs from those who remain below.

Those below may even know that they are in the wrong, but they are unwilling to do what they know deep down is required. They love luxury, fantasy, and pleasure. They do not want to live for Another. Instead, they desire to live for themselves.

In living for themselves, they choose to suppress the Truth. Eventually, this suppression leads to damnation. The call is no longer heard. The conviction is no longer battled or wrestled. Those who remain on ground level remain as they are. They will not change or seek to transform. Instead, they are continually being conformed into the world.

This sad, delusional state leads them to do the only thing they can do in this life – attempt to fulfill all they want while simultaneously hating those who have chosen to live for Him Who is Everlasting Life.

When we are hoisted upon the cross, our view goes from being towards the Heavens, seeing the hope set before us, to our head hanging low. This short time that seems to be prolonged has us excited for what is to come but also curious, sometimes unsure, and afraid.

The transition is glorious, but when we prepare ourselves to receive the Holy Spirit, there may be a brief hint of uncertainty, timidness, or fear. This is normal, as what is to come shall forever change us. We long for a better life but fear what Him Who is Life will demand from us.

The greatest transition known to man is to go from being a wicked heathen to a holy vessel for Christ. Much occurs throughout this transition. Forever, we grow in the knowledge of it — being seen as righteous because of what Christ has done, but continually growing in that righteousness while on earth. Perfection is not ours in this life, though the Father sees us as perfect because of Christ.

As we hang on the cross before men, we become exhausted. Our neck becomes tired and our limbs sore. We can barely move. Every breath is agonizing. We want to die. We are ready to die. Before we do, however, we look down at those of the world. Our heart feels for them because they still do not know what they do.

We desire that all would come by this way. For this is the test of true faith. The Cross is a Test of Truth. If we truly want to become born-again and a Disciple of Him Who rules Heaven and earth, we must go by way of the Cross.

Those unwilling to get on the cross live in a lukewarm state. This state damns many because many want to sit in their carnality and at the table with demons, seeking to invite God to the table. However, God does not come, for He is Holy and Just. He does not partake with those who embody evil, for God alone is Good. God alone is Wise. He will not bend or be tempted by evil. "Let no one say when he is tempted, "I am tempted by God"; for God cannot be tempted by evil, nor does He Himself tempt anyone" (James 1:13 NKJV).

A man who hangs on the cross is one whom others want to see hang and remain. They do not want to see a transitional death, but a stagnant death. If one desires to change and is willing to go to the cross, the world wants them to remain on the cross. They do not want to see someone be resurrected. Instead, they desire to see that person die in shame, agony, and defeat.

They want to see the man upon the cross die for nothing, for they love to see men fall. They are lovers of catastrophe and enjoy seeing others suffer for no cause. In Mark 15:6-15 (NKJV), Scripture tells us:

> "Now at the feast he was accustomed to releasing one prisoner to them, whomever they requested. And there was one named Barabbas, *who was* chained with his fellow rebels; they had committed murder in the rebellion. Then the multitude, crying aloud, began to ask *him to do* just as he had always done for them. But Pilate answered them, saying, "Do you want me to release to you the King of the Jews?" For he knew that the chief priests had handed Him over because of envy. But the chief priests stirred up the crowd, so that he should rather release Barabbas to them. Pilate answered and said to them again, "What then do you want me to do *with Him* whom you call the King of the Jews?" So they cried out again, "Crucify Him!" Then Pilate said to them, "Why, what evil has He done?" But they cried out all the more, "Crucify Him!" So Pilate, wanting to gratify the crowd, released Barabbas to them; and he delivered Jesus, after he had scourged *Him,* to be crucified."

The world gave up the Son of God for a murderer. Not

only did the world want to see the end of the Son of God, but Pilate also demonstrated cowardliness towards man's opinion.

Anyone swayed by man's opinions has no right to follow Christ. Anyone who would forsake the faith in giving the world what it desires is soft and weak. They are fearful of man and are willing to give up the Best for evil. That is why Scripture warns "The fear of man brings a snare, But whoever trusts in the LORD shall be safe" (Proverbs 29:25 NKJV).

The end of the Pharisees and Pilate is tragic. The Pharisees wanted to see a blameless man hang upon the Cross. Pilate did not want to be enemies with the world. Yet, we know that "For those who live according to the flesh set their minds on the things of the flesh, but those *who live* according to the Spirit, the things of the Spirit. For to be carnally minded *is* death, but to be spiritually minded *is* life and peace. Because the carnal mind *is* enmity against God; for it is not subject to the law of God, nor indeed can be" (Romans 8:5-7 NKJV). "Adulterers and adulteresses! Do you not know that friendship with the world is enmity with God? Whoever therefore wants to be a friend of the world makes himself an enemy of God" (James 4:4 NKJV).

Those who are carnal listen to the voices of those who are carnal more than God's. Those of God and those who are to come to know God are sensitive to the Spirit's conviction, drawing, and speaking.

Pilate was one who, although knew Christ was innocent and should not be crucified, gave in to the Pharisees. He wanted their approval rather than God's. He wanted a good reputation rather than standing up for what was right. This is the way of many who pretend to love Christ but are unwilling to die alongside Him.

We are commanded to abide in faith, hope, and love (1 Corinthians 13:13 NKJV). To receive God's unconditional love, we must first have faith that it is received through the Cross of Christ. This faith gives us a hope that cannot be defiled or perverted. By Christ's atoning sacrifice and our willingness to follow Him, we receive God's Love and are covered by the Blood.

The hope of eternal salvation and an eternity with God is found in Christ. Once faith has had its full effect after our death on the cross, this leads to a love of God and a love from God that can only be found and experienced in Christ.

Therefore, our faith must be active, not in its striving to earn salvation, but in its willingness to follow in the way of Him Who provided the way of salvation.

The world shall never understand, for how can they? "But the natural man does not receive the things of the Spirit of God, for they are foolishness to him; nor can he know *them,* because they are spiritually discerned" (1 Corinthians 2:14 NKJV). "For since, in the wisdom of God, the world through wisdom did not know God, it pleased God through the foolishness of the message preached to save those who believe. For Jews request a sign, and Greeks seek after wisdom; but we preach Christ crucified, to the Jews a stumbling block and to the Greeks foolishness, but to those who are called, both Jews and Greeks, Christ the power of God and the wisdom of God. Because the foolishness of God is wiser than men, and the weakness of God is stronger than men" (1 Corinthians 1:21-25 NKJV).

The Way of the Cross is foolishness to those who are perishing (1 Corinthians 1:18). To us who are being saved and are to be saved, it is the power of God.

The man hanging on the cross before the world is bound to receive what is unjust and maybe undeserved. At the same time, however, he shall receive what is from God and what is deserved.

This is the blessedness of hanging on the cross with Christ. We are not alone. For we worship and follow in the way of a Savior Who went through everything we are to go through, yet He was without sin. "For we do not have a High Priest who cannot sympathize with our weaknesses, but was in all *points* tempted as *we are, yet* without sin" (Hebrews 4:15 NKJV). Blessed be the name of the Lord Jesus Christ.

* * *

God of Glory, Who descended from realms by which we know not, Who loved us so much that His Son died for our sins, we worship You and give You praise. O God, give us the courage to hang before men upon our cross and face ridicule and torment, for it is better to face adversity from man than to face Your wrath. O Compassionate and Loving Father, be with us. Keep us from turning from the cross. Give us the fortitude to face all trials and difficulties from the world, God. Guide us into the great transition of being of this world to now only being in it. Bless us with Your touch, Holy Spirit. Teach us a new song to sing. May we give our all to You, for You have given us all things in Christ. In Jesus' name, Amen.

Quotes For Meditation

1. "Satan gives Adam an apple and takes away paradise. Therefore, in all temptations consider not what he offers, but what we shall lose." **Richard Sibbes**
2. "Even on the Cross He did not hide Himself from sight; rather, He made all creation witness to the presence of its Maker." **Athanasius of Alexandria**
3. "Christ's crucifixion was on a hill, by a road, where everybody who passed by could not only see His pain, but also His shame. It was not done in a shadow, hidden away somewhere." **Francis Schaeffer**
4. "The Gospel does not call us to receive Christ as an addition to our life, but as our life." **Paul Washer**
5. "If you wish to be like Christ, call or look always for the cross." **St. John of the Cross**

Chapter 18

Dying to Self & Sin

"For whoever desires to save his life will lose it, but whoever loses his life for My sake will save it." *Luke 9:24 NKJV*

Anyone can stand at the cross. Even the Pharisees and Romans saw Christ crucified. The difference between the religious heathens and the born-again believer is that the born-again believer does not merely look upon the cross of Christ; he gets on the cross with Christ, dying to self and sin.

A painful death scares away many from a genuine walk with Christ. Anyone can see what Christ has done. Anyone can buy into a man-made religion that comforts and does not challenge them. Even if there is a challenge in a specific religion, that challenge is not always to put away what is wrong. Instead, a man-made religion motivates others to do what is right.

"Be as good as you can, so long as you can, by the might and power of your hand." This is the way of the religious and the heathens who want to do good without knowing Him Who is Good.

Any religion or lifestyle that promotes goodness without repentance always ends in delusion and shame. Any faith that does not look to the Cross of Christ will not save. True faith comes from the disposition towards sin. This is what separates a true born-again believer from a self-proclaimed Christian.

Self-proclaimed Christians seek freedom *to* sin. True born-again believers seek freedom *from* sin. The difference between these people is found in one's willingness to die on the cross with Christ or to merely allow Christ to be the only One on the cross and neglect any call for us to die to sin and self. Of course, there is no such thing as perfection in this life. This reality, however, has brought about many excuses within the Christian community.

Many believe that because we cannot reach perfection in this life, progress and growth are not required. Those who have such a view are lazy and conceited. They desire all that Christ gives without listening to His commandments. They claim to love Him but continue in the very thing that crucified Him. This path is both tragic and lacks any fear of the Lord. This path leads to damnation disguised by a false banner of love.

That is why "Jesus said to His disciples, "If anyone desires to come after Me, let him deny himself, and take up his cross, and follow Me"" (Matthew 16:24 NKJV). The call to be crucified and die to sin and self helps to reveal the wheat from the chaff. It directly penetrates the heart of every man and exposes their true willingness to have a repentant faith or a mere professing faith.

Anyone can say, "Yes, I believe Christ came down to earth and died for my sins." People can claim the Cross and say, "I accept Jesus is Lord, and He did what was required upon that cross for me to go to Heaven." They accept all these things as if they were checkboxes and continue going their way. They have the correct answers, but their feet make haste to fulfill sin. There is no desire to turn, change, repent, and be transformed. There is no desire to die to that which sent Christ to the Cross.

If we do not die to sin and self, we will not resurrect like The King and Lord Who is over all. We will die an eternal death. One where we are forever living but always dying. This is what we know to be Hell.

The path of a born-again believer is to humbly carry their cross to the top of the hill. The true born-again believer will possess a holy desire to set their cross next to Christ's and to truly want to die to self as they are nailed to the cross, putting to death any lifestyle of sin. This, in return, leads them to be resurrected into newness of life. For *"There is* therefore now no condemnation to those who are in Christ Jesus, who do not walk according to the flesh, but according to the Spirit. For the law of the Spirit of life in Christ Jesus has made me free from the law of sin and death" (Romans 8:1-2 NKJV).

Freedom is found in Christ alone. Not freedom to *sin*, but freedom to *live*. Not freedom to live as we desire, but based on God's direction and counsel. For He is a Good and Faithful God. He wants to bless His children and be with them. He longs for us to live in the freedom of His Son's atoning sacrifice, distance ourselves from sin, and die to self.

Those who continue in the way of their sin and selfishness will never be free. For liberty to do as one pleases does not always bring freedom. Man may be free to go to-and-fro where he pleases, but where he leads himself can guide him into devastating consequences. An example of this is prison.

Many had the freedom to do something, only to find them-selves caught and facing the consequences and penalties of their actions. Depending on the crime, reputations are ruined, job opportunities diminished, and even seeing the world is entirely dissolved. God can redeem such men who go to prison, but the consequences of what was done beforehand shall remain. Not in God's eyes, as "He is faithful and just to forgive us *our* sins and to cleanse us from all unrighteousness" (1 John 1:9 NKJV). However, the consequences of how we are perceived and bound by the world may forever remain, though they do not define us.

This is to say that just because people have the freedom to live for themselves and live in sin does not mean they are truly free. Their freedom is bondage. Their freedom used in an ungodly manner is digging their own grave. They are slowly preparing themselves for Hell. They are unwilling to turn. In being free, they have become their own slave. However, for us who know God, we have become a slave so that we might become free.

2 Peter 2:18-21 (NKJV) warns of the deception of false prophets:

"For when they speak great swelling *words* of emptiness, they allure through the lusts of the flesh, through lewdness, the ones who have actually escaped from those who live in error. While they promise them liberty, they themselves are slaves of corruption; for by whom a person is overcome, by him also he is brought into bondage. For if, after they have escaped the pollutions of the world through the knowledge of the Lord and Savior Jesus Christ, they are again entangled in them and overcome, the latter end is worse for them than the beginning. For it would have been better for them not to have known the way of righteousness, than having known *it*, to turn from the holy commandment delivered to them."

True freedom is submission to God. True liberty is by way of the cross. Death to sin and self must occur if we are to truly enter the freedom, blessing, glory, riches, knowledge, and understanding of Christ and His atoning sacrifice. Without a willingness to die to self, we shall not live.

Again, this death is a daily death. It is not a one-time act that dictates the rest of our lives. Continually, we must seek to be delivered from ourselves. Though we are saved by the genuineness of our decision to die to sin and self, this does not negate the reality that we must continually monitor our steps. There will be a spiritual battle every hour of every day.

The Enemy will attack us, the world will tempt us, people will persecute us, and even those closest to us will ridicule us. Thoughts of doubt and fear of whether or not it is worth following Christ may loom and be planted in our minds. We must not give way to such feelings and thoughts, however.

The path of the true born-again believer was never meant to be easy. It is a path of sacrifice. Not sacrificing to God to *earn our salvation* but sacrificing our carnality in *working out our salvation*. Those willing to fight and wage war against self and sin shall forever reside under Him, the Alpha and the Omega.

A heroic soul goes to war to defend his nation and family. A godly soul wages war against his passions and lusts to keep his sanctity and purity.

We know that "those *who are* Christ's have crucified the flesh with its passions and desires" (Galatians 5:24 NKJV). Continually, we can wage war daily in the power of the Spirit. It is a bloody war. It is a spiritual war. It is a holy war! The righteousness of Christ equips us for every good work! The Armor of God prepares us for every spiritual attack! God Almighty shall be with us, but we must be willing to die to sin and self.

May God give us the strength to endure this painful death. Though this death prepares us to receive the Holy Spirit, this death shall continue to occur day by day. We will never not need to wage war against self and sin. Each day will present new battles, struggles, and temptations. We must be willing to fight to the very end.

Just as Christ said in Matthew 24:13 (NKJV), "he who endures to the end shall be saved."

* * *

God of Wonder and Glory, Who created the only Way of salvation, Who sent His Son to die upon the Cross for our sins, You are Righteous and Just. Your mercies are new every morning. You are the One and Only God Who cannot lie. O God, may we see what Christ did upon the Cross. Deepen our understanding and revelation of that Great and Mighty act! For there is no better story than Your Story. There is no glory that is not Yours! You are worthy of all things. O God, give us the strength to die to sin and self each day. May we not entertain the things of this life. Help us to do what is right. Give us the ability to face adversity and remain humble in times of prosperity. Help us not to allow the things of this life to dim the Light within. O Holy Spirit, we desire that You would be lively within! May we have the courage to hang upon our cross and die alongside Christ. May we prepare ourselves to be reborn. May we take the full blow of conviction and truly die, that we might live not only in the Heaven to come, but that Heaven may come to live in us now. In Jesus' name, Amen.

Quotes For Meditation

1. "Revival is a renewed conviction of sin and repentance, followed by an intense desire to live in obedience to God. It is giving up one's will to God in deep humility." **Charles Finney**

2. "You do wrong to complain of your crosses and sufferings. Believe me, you know not what it is to suffer." **Paul of the Cross**

3. "God never negotiates with men. Jesus Christ's death on the cross put an end to any kind of negotiations. It is now Christ or nothing. It is now God's Word in Its entirety or nothing." **A.W. Tozer**

4. "The cross is going to judge everything in your life: your eating, your drinking, your sleeping, your spending, your talking. Everything is cross-examined!" **Leonard Ravenhill**

5. "There was a day when I died; died to self, my opinions, preferences, tastes and will; died to the

world, its approval or censure; died to the approval or blame even of my brethren or friends; and since then I have studied only to show myself approved unto God." **George Muller**

Chapter 19

Despised & Rejected

"Then two robbers were crucified with Him, one on the right and another on the left. And those who passed by blasphemed Him, wagging their heads and saying, "You Who destroy the temple and build it in three days, save Yourself! If You are the Son of God, come down from the cross."" *Matthew 27:38-40 NKJV*

A man on a cross will forever be despised and rejected.

Anyone who goes to the cross will automatically be one the world hates and condemns. There is no acceptance of a man who resides upon a cross. There is no desire to befriend a man upon a cross. For the cross signifies one who must suffer and who is cursed.

Those on the cross will be judged by self-righteous individuals unwilling to yield to the sin-exposing conviction of the Holy Spirit. Those inflated with ego and pride cannot see that they, too, must go by way of the cross. However, they remain where they are in their delusion, condemning and mocking those upon the cross.

To be despised by others is to be hated for doing what others are unwilling to do. When it comes to preparing ourselves to know God, others will do all they can to try and convince themselves that they are in the right and we are in the wrong. They will develop for themselves all kinds of fantasies and stories. Instead of understanding the faith and the true call of Christ Jesus, they deliberately refuse to listen to the instructions of the Lord. They claim something as if they knew it, only to prevent themselves from submitting to God and experiencing Him.

This is the way of all unrepentant sinners. They will despise those who are bold enough to die on the cross. They will forever remain at a distance or directly nearby and will be unwilling to bend their knee to God. Rather than seeing *why* we are upon the cross, they see *only us* on the cross.

They see us as deserving their ridicule, mocking, scoffing, despising, and rejection. They see us as one who is not of them. Glory be to God, we are not one of them, for we are preparing ourselves for that which is too wonderful for word and too lofty for the carnal mind to understand.

When Christ was crucified, the people mocked Him, "saying, "If You are the King of the Jews, save Yourself"" (Luke 23:37 NKJV). Anyone who desires to live for God will hear similar echoes. They will say, "If God is so Great and Mighty, then why doesn't He (fill in the blank)." Just as the people mocked Christ directly for Who He was and what He claimed to be, so people will ridicule us for our belief in Christ.

When we hang upon the Cross with Christ, people will not only despise us, but our faith will be ridiculed. The name of Christ will be blasphemed amongst unrepentant sinners. They will give false claims and make uneducated judgments about the faith. They will scoff at Christ and think we are insane to dedicate our lives to Him. Amid their depraved states, they cannot see the Truth or transformation of what is taking place.

No man goes willingly to the cross who does not already agree with its consequences. For the believer, we go willingly to the Cross because we not only see our Savior there, but we see the hope of what is to come. "For our light affliction, which is but for a moment, is working for us a far more exceeding *and* eternal weight of glory, while we do not look at the things which are seen, but at the things which are not seen. For the things which are seen *are* temporary, but the things which are not seen *are* eternal" (2 Corinthians 4:17-18 NKJV).

Pain is temporary. Glory with God is eternal. Not glory for our sake, but to live under the glory of Him Who deserves all the glory. For God alone deserves all that is because He has made all that is.

When we willingly go to the cross, be crucified, and die upon it, we shall truly see God in a new light. We will not see God as a "moral monster" or "a flying spaghetti man" as so many Atheists enjoy giving God these titles of blasphemy. No, we will see God for Who He is.

The death of a person upon a cross is not only physical but metaphysical. Our minds and hearts are darkened. We do not know God or seek God, naturally. We are continually corrupt within. Though all sins range, they are rampant without Holy Ghost conviction. However, when we have the Holy Ghost within, He is the Gift that is received by our metaphysical death. The mind naturally wanders in selfish, lustful, and prideful directions. The mind does not want to acknowledge the reproof of another or turn from that which it fantasizes and enjoys. Receiving the Holy Spirit requires a metaphysical death upon the cross and an internal mortification.

There are many religions and denominations that claim

Christ but do not follow Him. Any path that focuses on external crucifixion, but not internal crucifixion, is merely putting on a show. They purposely wound and hurt themselves to "suffer with Christ". However, this is not the way of God. For God does not desire that we harm ourselves. This is the path of those who are deranged. Though suffering will come, it must be permitted by God to happen to us.

There is no commandment to inflict self-harm upon ourselves. Instead, we are called to be internally crucified. This means a willingness to forsake and mortify all that is contrary to God. It means dying to all carnality and admitting that our internal state needs a Holy Purge from Him Who is Holy.

Therefore, people may seek to be crucified externally. It may make for a good show and a false sense of security by unnecessary suffering. Ultimately, however, it is vanity if one is not willing to be metaphysically crucified within. For many may brag and claim the name of Christ. Many will say they suffer so much externally, but if they are unwilling to let go of what is still harbored within, the suffering and external crucifixion is still led by self and not by God.

For us who are truly born-again, "we have this treasure in earthen vessels, that the excellence of the power may be of God and not of us. *We are* hard-pressed on every side, yet not crushed; *we are* perplexed, but not in despair; persecuted, but not forsaken; struck down, but not destroyed— always carrying about in the body the dying of the Lord Jesus, that the life of Jesus also may be manifested in our body. For we who live are always delivered to death for Jesus' sake, that the life of Jesus also may be manifested in our mortal flesh. So then death is working in us, but life in you" (2 Corinthians 4:7-12 NKJV).

Amid evil, we can be "strengthened with all might, according to His glorious power, for all patience and longsuffering with joy" (Colossians 1:11 NKJV). We don't have to be afraid of the external and internal death that is to take place. Though the world will despise us for hanging upon the cross, we despise ourselves within. The world may even be right in its ridicule (if it is congruent with how we see ourselves), for we know our depraved state. We know what we have held onto for too long. We know what has been an idol ahead of God. We understand what sins have been part of our lifestyle. We know what our viewpoint has been towards other people. We know the internal secrets within the chambers of our hearts, and if the world ridicules us for such things, then let them. All the more reason we must die.

If the world sees what we see, we know it must go. However, if the world despises us simply because we are willing to go in the opposite direction of them, so be it.

May we patiently endure their judgment. For the Truth of Christ will be revealed in time. We need not worry about our lives; we are ready to die. We need not wonder what is to occur, for this is the way of those near the path of eternal life.

Not all pain has a purpose, but purpose can be worked out through the pain. Some pain is meant for our good. Other pain is self-induced and self-inflicted. It takes a willingness to go in the way of God for all pain to have the potential and opportunity of eternal meaning and reward. For suffering for Christ is never in vain. Suffering for the sake of the Gospel is a blessing that not many can partake in. Though it is offered to all, many are too weak to endure that which God declares will occur to those who follow Him.

"So Pilate gave sentence that it should be as they requested. And he released to them the one they requested, who for rebellion and murder had been thrown into prison; but he delivered Jesus to their will. Now as they led Him away, they laid hold of a certain man, Simon a Cyrenian, who was coming from the country, and on him they laid the cross that he might bear *it* after Jesus. And a great multitude of the people followed Him, and women who also mourned and lamented Him. But Jesus, turning to them, said, "Daughters of Jerusalem, do not weep for Me, but weep for yourselves and for your children" (Luke 23:24-28 NKJV). Those who go in the way of Christ must weep for their own. For as they transition, they shall see multitudes unwilling to follow. Not unwilling to follow them but unwilling to follow the True path that leads to Eternal Life.

When we aim to grow and move towards the things of God, many will remain stagnant. This is the difference from those unwilling to get on the cross. Not only do they not see themselves as needing to get on the cross, but they are also reluctant to be a spectacle for Someone outside themselves. They want others to see them as they are, based upon who they are, apart from God. They put on a false perception. The irony is that the one who is on the cross is the one who gains everyone's attention. They are those that others see, monitor, and follow—not following in the sense of being led to being nailed to a cross but following how this person turns out. People will be curious to see if there is a spiritual awakening and internal resurrection of the one who dies on the cross.

Therefore, those who choose to die on the cross, though despised and ridiculed, will be monitored by those who hate them. Those who hate are those who follow those whom they hate. They have no freedom. Their anger and envy desire to monitor every movement of those they despise. Amidst this, if we abide in Christ, they shall see the living proof of God within that cannot be denied. They, amid their ungodly motives, will be humbled. They will see that which they do not want to see.

Just as God works evil out for a greater good (Genesis 50:20), He can take the wicked motives of unbelievers and work it out in such a way that they are without excuse. Those who cannot give up the want of seeing God's people fail will see God's faithfulness come forth. Their impurity will reveal the Pure One within the believer. As others hate those willing to humble themselves before God and follow Him, they shall see that Christianity is the one true faith.

There is no other hope. There is no other way. Only through the cross does a man prove his desire for God, his hatred for sin, and his willingness to change.

May God help us live our lives so that those who despise and ridicule us are reproved and humbled by the resurrected life that is to come. May we patiently endure the suffering God permits in our lives.

If we were not striving for and living a life that convicted those in the darkness, we would also be darkened vessels. Thanks be to God, however, that the Truth of His Word, His Spirit, and His Being is made evident. May we endure the world's rejection in understanding that they are vessels validating we are on the right path.

"Therefore we also, since we are surrounded by so great a cloud of witnesses, let us lay aside every weight, and the sin which so easily ensnares *us,* and let us run with endurance the race that is set before us, looking unto Jesus, the Author and Finisher of *our* faith, Who for the joy that was set before Him endured the cross, despising the shame, and has sat down at the right hand of the throne of God" (Hebrews 12:1-2 NKJV).

* * *

O God of Light and Truth, Him Who loves all He has created and desires mercy, blessed Art Thou. You alone, O God, provided the way of salvation. Give us the strength to endure being despised and rejected by those in darkness. O God, fill our hearts with compassion towards those on their way to Hell. May

145

we pray for them, love them, and turn the other cheek when they harm us. Give us wisdom and discernment in understanding that our death is a glorious one. Christ, You suffered for our sake because of Your love for us. May we endure suffering that is permitted by You for Your glory. May we not become discouraged or find it strange when the day's trials come. For You promise these things will occur. God, we patiently endure the world's wrath, hatred, and anger. May we have the peace, patience, and gentleness of our Lord and Savior. Be glorified, O Holy One Whose Love abounds. In Jesus' name, Amen.

Quotes For Meditation

1. "By a beautiful paradox of Divine love, God makes His Cross the very means of our salvation and our life. We have slain Him; we have nailed Him there and crucified Him; but the Love in His eternal heart could not be extinguished. He willed to give us the very life we slew; to give us the very Food we destroyed; to nourish us with the very Bread we buried, and the very Blood we poured forth. He made our very crime into a happy fault; He turned a Crucifixion into a Redemption; a Consecration into a Communion; a death into Life Everlasting." **Fulton J. Sheen**

2. "The Cross to me is certain salvation. The Cross is that which I ever adore. The Cross of the Lord is with me. The Cross is my refuge." **Thomas Aquinas**

3. "Being disguised under the disfigurement of an ugly crucifixion and death, the Christ upon the

cross is paradoxically the clearest revelation of Who God is." **Hans Urs von Balthasar**

4. "Meditation on Jesus Christ crucified is a precious balm which sweetens all pains." **Paul of the Cross**

5. "The earthly form of Christ is the form that died on the cross. The image of God is the image of Christ crucified. It is to this image that the life of the disciples must be conformed; in other words, they must be conformed to His death (Phil 3.10, Rom 6.4). The Christian life is a life of crucifixion (Gal 2.19). In baptism the form of Christ's death is impressed upon His own. They are dead to the flesh and to sin, they are dead to the world, and the world is dead to them (Gal 6.14). Anybody living in the strength of Christ's baptism lives in the strength of Christ's death." **Dietrich Bonhoeffer**

Chapter 20

Dying on the Cross with Christ

"S o when Jesus had received the sour wine, He said, "It is finished!" And bowing His head, He gave up His spirit." John 19:30 NKJV

When a man dies on the cross, everything has been extracted. Judgment has been finished, and never again will that man be judged. He has endured the suffering and persecution of the world. These fires test whether a man's soon-to-be faith is genuine and real or just an instant burst of emotion or desire to believe. For true faith will continue and will endure. It will not recoil or forsake God. True faith stands the test and faces what lies ahead.

A man who willingly dies to sin and self shall forever live with Christ. When our final death comes, we will be brought into the Heavenly realms. We will be illuminated within with the Holy Spirit.

The Spirit quickly comes to the repentant heart that has died to self and the world. The Spirit is readily equipped to flood our souls with a rebirth! We are to be born-again, and God's Way is the only way to be born-again. We must die with Christ on the cross to truly receive life beyond the cross. For death upon the Cross for Christ led to resurrected life. In return, anyone who goes in the way of our Blessed Lord and Savior shall receive the same.

"Now when the sixth hour had come, there was darkness over the whole land until the ninth hour" (Mark 15:33 NKJV). Before a man's death upon a cross, it always gets the darkest. Loneliness sets in. Pain and agony are felt. Discouragement and fear take place. All these emotions and feelings, however, are what lead man to think beyond himself. All these dispositions and states lead to the darkness that will soon be overcome by the Light. For the darkness that sweeps over us is one final attack from the Enemy (in so far as preventing us from becoming born-again).

The Enemy will do anything and everything to cloud our judgment and view. He will whisper lies and tempt us to turn from the way in which we are going. Little does he know that those nailed to a cross never get down early from the cross. Those who have come to the point of being on the cross shall remain there until their final death.

"Now there stood by the cross of Jesus His mother, and His mother's sister, Mary the *wife* of Clopas, and Mary Magdalene. When Jesus therefore saw His mother, and the disciple whom He loved standing by, He said to His mother, "Woman, behold your son!"" (John 19:25-26 NKJV). When darkness sweeps over the one who is to receive a transformation, all others are watching and witnessing. For Christ, His mother saw Him in agony and pain, taking on the total weight of sin and the full blow of God's wrath.

For us, the world shall see the pain and struggle against ourselves. We have no one to fight when on the cross. We have gone to die, and our death is entirely correlated to us. We are there not because of what someone else did or has done. We are on the Cross solely by what we have done.

Those who play the victim and are unwilling to listen to the reproof of God will not be converted. They will continue to go their own way, unwilling to allow the Power of God to change them. Those, however, who hang on the cross are not playing games. They have refrained from excuses. They don't want to remain as they are. No matter how painful, they are willing to die an excruciating death. For they know that Christ is beside them. He has gone before them. They are not alone. They are accompanied by the Great and Wonderful King of kings and Lord of lords.

Mark 15:20-32 (NKJV) reminds us of why Christ was brought to the point of hanging on the Cross and what accusation was against Him. Scripture states:

> "And when they had mocked Him, they took the purple off Him, put His own clothes on Him, and led Him out to crucify Him. Then they compelled a certain man, Simon a Cyrenian, the father of Alexander and Rufus, as he was coming out of the country and passing by, to bear His cross. And they brought Him to the place Golgotha, which is translated, Place of a Skull. Then they gave Him wine mingled with myrrh to drink, but He did not take *it*. And when they crucified Him, they divided His garments, casting lots for them *to determine* what every man should take. Now it was the third hour, and they crucified Him. And the inscription of His accusation was written above: THE KING OF THE JEWS. With Him they also crucified two robbers, one on His right and the other on His left. So the Scripture was fulfilled which says, "And He was numbered with the transgressors." And those who passed by blasphemed Him, wagging their heads and saying, "Aha! *You* who destroy the temple and build *it* in three days, save Yourself, and come down from the cross!" Likewise the chief priests also, mocking among themselves with the scribes, said, "He saved others; Himself He cannot save. Let the Christ, the King of Israel, descend now from the cross,

that we may see and believe." Even those who were crucified with Him reviled

Him."

Amid His death, Christ was Faithful, Pure, and Loving to the very end. He did not revoke His call. He did not seek to justify Himself before man. He did not try to argue His way down from the Cross. He did not complain about His current situation. He willingly endured the Cross and paid the penalty that all of us deserved.

Though we follow Christ by way of the Cross, we do not have to go through a physical death on the cross. He took upon Himself all that was evil and sinful. Somehow, the Perfect and Pure One became sin for us. God "made Him who knew no sin *to be* sin for us, that we might become the righteousness of God in Him" (2 Corinthians 5:21 NKJV).

"And Jesus cried out with a loud voice, and breathed His last. Then the veil of the temple was torn in two from top to bottom. So when the centurion, who stood opposite Him, saw that He cried out like this and breathed His last, he said, "Truly this Man was the Son of God!"" (Mark 15:37-39 NKJV). When Christ breathed His last, even his enemies admitted He was the Son of God.

Those who crucified Him and were near Him during His death acknowledged that what they were witnessing was not just a random man hanging on the cross. No, this was the God-incarnate man. God in the flesh — the One Who God sent into the world that the world might be saved through Him (John 3:17).

When a glorious death occurs from one about to enter newness of life, a final goodbye to lifestyles is said. A transition of joy and peace never experienced is soon to occur. Most will desire us to be miserable and remain dead on the cross. However, all will be watching what is to take place.

Those who watch our death may even leave after thinking that what has been done has been done. They may think it was all a waste and we lost our minds. They may think we have chosen the wrong way and intentionally suppressed our desires and passions for no reason. They may believe that the most significant loss is losing them as friends.

Whatever they may say, think, or do after our death is of no concern to us. We are not to judge those outside the church when we are soon to be brought into the Church. For Scripture tells us in 1 Corinthians 5:12-13 (NKJV), "For what *have* I *to do* with judging those also who are outside? Do you not judge those who are inside? But those who are outside God judges. Therefore "put away from yourselves the evil person.""

"But one of the soldiers pierced His side with a spear, and immediately blood and water came out" (John 19:34 NKJV). The proof that we have just died is in the recognition that the blood of the flesh and the water of the Spirit is revealed. What was only blood now has the Spirit. This was proof that Christ had the Holy Spirit within Him. He had the Baptism of the Holy Ghost. For us who die, our blood shall be drained, but we shall be filled with the Living Water.

The Holy Ghost can move in as soon as we are drained from the things of this world, and we bleed out our last of sin and self — not in perfect conduct, but in the perfect desire to be delivered from that which the wicked and unrepentant sinners take part in without any desire to change. When our intention and motive are pure, the Holy Spirit discerns the authenticity of our intention and motive and rushes in. Like a whirlwind, we are quickly filled and transformed within.

This is why we must know that "He who believes and is baptized will be saved; but he who does not believe will be condemned" (Mark 16:16 NKJV). True belief leads to a true death. A true death is a validation that we truly believe. This is the proof that the greatest death of all can convert us. For Christ's death is the only one that both was resurrected and offered newness of life to all, freely.

May we come to see the blessedness of dying. As we hang on the cross before all, may they see us die. May we take in the full blow of all that is to come. May we patiently endure all that is convicting and agonizing. For this is only temporary. In due time, we shall be made new. That time happens at the point of our last breath on the cross. When this occurs, we are ready to go through the Cross.

Let us endure the cross to the very end and endure the road of the newness of life that is to come. For ""he who endures to the end shall be saved"" (Matthew 24:13 NKJV).

* * *

O God of Glory, Who has blessed man with the gift of salvation and the power of the Spirit, may we endure our death upon the Cross patiently and willingly. O God, may the great transformation take place within. May we turn from our wicked ways and repent of our sins before You. May we hide under the shadow of Your Cross. May we be forever covered by the Blood. O God, give us strength and courage to endure the blow of the world and Your conviction. Though theirs is in spite and hate, Yours is in love. May we forever live to magnify You. Prepare us now to go through the Cross, that our old ways may be gone, as we put on the new. In Jesus' name, Amen.

Quotes For Meditation

1. "Come, and see the victories of the cross. Christ's wounds are thy healings, His agonies thy repose, His conflicts thy conquests, His groans thy songs, His pains thine ease, His shame thy glory, His death thy life, His sufferings thy salvation."
Matthew Henry

2. "God proved His love on the Cross. When Christ hung, and held, and died, it was God saying to the world, 'I love you.'" **Billy Graham**

3. "When Jesus Christ shed His blood on the cross, it was not the blood of a martyr; or the blood of one man for another; it was the life of God poured out to redeem the world." **Oswald Chambers**

4. "Let us cling to the Cross, placing all our hopes on the Cross, so that taught through the Cross, fixing our thought on Heaven, being brought close to Christ our Savior, we may be found worthy to be near God in the Kingdom of Heaven, in Christ our

Lord Himself, to Whom be glory and might to the ages of ages. Amen." **John Chrysostom**

5. "All those who belong to Jesus Christ are fastened with Him to the cross." **St. Augustine**

Part Five

Through The Cross

Chapter 21

Through The Cross

"Long-lasting victory can never be separated from a long-lasting stand on the foundation of the Cross." Watchman Nee

The path of the Disciple of Christ is by the Cross, to the Cross, and through the Cross. Without a true death, one cannot experience true life. Without willingly enduring all that comes by way of the cross, we will never truly be transformed by the work of Christ on the cross. For the power of Christ on the Cross does not change, only our ability to receive its power. The lack of transformation is not on God's end but ours.

When a person chooses to die on their cross alongside Christ, they are raised into newness of life. "Therefore, if anyone *is* in Christ, *he is* a new creation; old things have passed away; behold, all things have become new" (2 Corinthians 5:17 NKJV). When we go through the Cross, we become that which could otherwise not be obtained.

By our flesh, we die. By the Spirit, we live. We are physically alive, yet spiritually dead without the Holy Spirit. With the Holy Spirit, we are both physically and spiritually alive. We live not with Earth's values but with eternity's values in view. We strive to "seek first the kingdom of God and His right-eousness", knowing that "all these things shall be added to you" (Matthew 6:33 NKJV).

Those who stand on the foundations of the Cross are those who have gone through the Cross. They have counted the cost and are no longer lost. They strive in the way of Christ, being renewed, sanctified, purified, and restored each day.

All that is to come by way of the Cross is painful initially but glorious in the ending. If we are willing to endure the fire that tries us, we shall receive the fruits of Him Who saved us. Just as fruits cannot grow without a tree, a Christian cannot bear fruits without first dying upon the tree.

The cross resembles all of life. As we go through the Cross, we shall be transformed and changed into a new creature, resurrected into newness of life, understand that suffering is the road to glory, and receive a promised hope of salvation. May God grant us the ability to see the many blessings that are both undeserved and received when we go through the Cross.

Chapter 22

Transformed & Changed into a New Creature

"*And you, being dead in your trespasses and the uncircumcision of your flesh, He has made alive together with Him, having forgiven you all trespasses, having wiped out the handwriting of requirements that was against us, which was contrary to us. And He has taken it out of the way, having nailed it to the cross. Having disarmed principalities and powers, He made a public spectacle of them, triumphing over them in it.*" *Colossians 2:13-15 NKJV*

In Christ alone are Life and Liberty. He is the Basis and Foundation of these blessed gifts.

There is nothing outside God that can transform man for the better. No resource, connection, system, or group can change a man into a new creature. The basis of this new creature is not in fixing a habit or getting rid of one bad thing. It is a revolution against the soul where man is purified within and seen as new without.

Humans are perceptive. We can sense and see the differences that occur between certain individuals. Though many have different levels of perception, all of us can see when change is taking place with someone we know. We see their habits shift. We hear the difference in their speech. We observe their actions. All of these can be noticed among all people who seek to change.

Those who have the Holy Spirit are those who are new creatures. They are no longer the same as they once were. Now, their very presence is differentiated from their former. The born-again believer does not merely change based upon subtle shifts but through an entire transformation.

When we become covered by the Blood, we are those who now go through the Cross. No longer are we slaves to this world but slaves to God. The liberty found under the Banner of God's Love has moved us into a promised, glorified state. Though this state cannot come to full fruition in this life, it can nonetheless be moved towards that glorified state through the work of sanctification. For although people help on a one-at-a-time focus level, the Holy Spirit focuses on the collectivity of our being. He does not merely work on one area and considers us as new. He will get rid of the essentials that must go and then convict us on deeper levels as we mature in the faith.

All the Holy Spirit does is for the benefit of our entire being, and a transformation of being is considered changing into a new creature. We cannot eliminate one thing and call ourselves a new creature. Only the Holy Spirit can sanctify the entirety of our being. This comes with conviction from sin, new convictions about life, new hopes, dreams, desires, ambitions, and a new way of life!

Only Christ can provide the way for us to be transformed and changed into new creatures. For just as Romans 5:12-19 (NKJV) declares:

"Therefore, just as through one man sin entered the world, and death through sin, and thus death spread to all men, because all sinned— (For until the law sin was in the world, but sin is not imputed when there is no law. Nevertheless death reigned from Adam to Moses, even over those who had not sinned according to the likeness of the transgression of Adam, who is a type of Him who was to come. But the free gift *is* not like the offense. For if by the one man's offense many died, much more the grace of God and the gift by the grace of the one Man, Jesus Christ, abounded to many. And the gift *is* not like *that which came* through the one who sinned. For the judgment *which came* from one *offense resulted* in condemnation, but the free gift *which came* from many offenses *resulted* in justification. For if by the one man's offense death reigned through the one, much more those who receive abundance of grace and of the gift of righteousness will reign in life through the One, Jesus Christ.) Therefore, as through one man's offense *judgment came* to all men, resulting in condemnation, even so through one Man's righteous act *the free gift came* to all men, resulting in justification of life. For as by one man's disobedience many were made sinners, so also by one Man's obedience many will be made righteous."

Man was originally made perfect but utilized his natural free will to go against God. Christ, Who was Perfect, has made us be seen as perfect by the Father based on what He has done. His Glorious Act upon the Cross changes us from wretched sinners into righteous saints.

The Glow of the Holy Ghost within is offered and given because of Christ's actions. No longer does God see an endless void of eternal darkness within. Instead, He now sees His Light within, shining throughout the crevasses of our souls.

This is the beautiful reality of going through the Cross and being transformed. What was once dark within us is now Light. "For you were once darkness, but now *you are* light in the Lord. Walk as children of light (for the fruit of the Spirit *is* in all goodness, righteousness, and truth), finding out what is acceptable to the Lord" (Ephesians 5:8-10 NKJV). When God's Light is within, we are born-again. When His Spirit resides, we have confirmation of new life. He is the Seal and Proof that we are new creatures.

A man can change only so much on his own. A man can attempt to do good while his spiritual side remains in darkness. It is only God Who can change us within. It is only God Who can have the physical, visible change manifested because of the spiritual change. Any change that is physical and visible to the human eye, but does not consist of a spiritual change within, is vanity.

"And I, brethren, when I came to you, did not come with excellence of speech or of wisdom declaring to you the testimony of God. For I determined not to know anything among you except Jesus Christ and Him crucified. I was with you in weakness, in fear, and in much trembling. And my speech and my preaching *were* not with persuasive words of human wisdom, but in demonstration of the Spirit and of power, that your faith should not be in the wisdom of men but in the power of God" (1 Corinthians 2:1-5 NKJV).

True faith happens in the power of the Spirit, not eloquence of speech. A man may be well-read, but spiritually dead if he is not feasting on the Eternal Bread; namely, God's Holy Word. Only God's Spirit can bring the greatest transformation known to man. Anyone who depends upon others or themselves to change is a slave to idolatry or seduced by deception. For the Enemy works in more ways than one, yet his end goal remains forever the same — to keep us from being transformed into children of the Light and seeking to know, love, serve, and glorify God.

The sad reality is that, because of the Enemy and man's own doing, many are deceived into thinking they *are* part of the faith simply because they *partake* in the things of the faith. Many in the pews are sitting at the foot of the Cross, but they are unwilling to go through the Cross. Many are willing to hear what Christ has done but do not want to listen to the call of what they must do.

Faith is active. We are not saved by what we do, but what we do is part of what leads us to enter into the faith. Without a deliberate decision to choose the things of God and deny ourselves, faith is merely in word. It is merely accepted by the head but does not transform the heart.

Those who truly know God and experience Him are those who chose to lay down their sin. They sought after the power of God to change them, not hearing what God had to say and attempting to change themselves. For many seek to make their way to Heaven by way of themselves, which is impossible. It is all done by God and for God. With this in mind, we come to understand that we have a "middle decision" of choosing to accept or reject Christ and believing or ignoring His Word, based on the amount of Truth presented to us by God. Our "middle decision" is between what God presents to us and whether or not He sends His Spirit. We have a "middle decision" to respond authentically and genuinely to His call.

"For God so loved the world that He gave His only begotten Son, that whoever believes in Him should not perish but have everlasting life" (John 3:16 NKJV). God loves all and is calling all. Sadly, not all respond to His call. Therefore, God chooses only some.

Those who choose to respond to the call are in for a painful road. As we have covered, few there be who follow in the way of the Cross.

No one has trouble looking upon a cross, but to get on the cross is another matter altogether. No one has a problem seeing others crucified, but when the call to die to self is had, many become too prideful, fearful, or involved with the world. Only those willing to live the crucified life shall enter into newness of life.

Christ "is our peace, Who has made both one, and has broken down the middle wall of separation, having abolished in His flesh the enmity, *that is,* the law of commandments *contained* in ordinances, so as to create in Himself one new man *from* the two, *thus* making peace, and that He might reconcile them both to God in one body through the cross, thereby putting to death the enmity" (Ephesians 2:14-16 NKJV).

True peace involves changing from that which is disruptive and distorted. True transformation leads to peace because it entails a distancing from what is not of God and contrary to God. In return, this change is revealed in the entirety of who we are. For our identity is no longer in ourselves and what we do but in Christ.

"For if we have been united together in the likeness of His death, certainly we also shall be *in the likeness* of *His* resurrection, knowing this, that our old man was crucified with *Him,* that the body of sin might be done away with, that we should no longer be slaves of sin. For he who has died has been freed from sin. Now if we died with Christ, we believe that we shall also live with Him, knowing that Christ, having been raised from the dead, dies no more. Death no longer has dominion over Him. For *the death* that He died, He died to sin once for all; but *the life* that He lives, He lives to God. Likewise you also, reckon yourselves to be dead indeed to sin, but alive to God in Christ Jesus our Lord" (Romans 6:5-11 NKJV).

If we die with Christ on the Cross, we shall be resurrected with Him and go through the Cross. For those who die on the Cross, do not remain on the cross. They go through the Cross, readily equipped and prepared to reveal to the world that the Christian faith is the true faith.

The Christian life is the inner life. The God of the Holy Bible is the One, True God. Resurrection brings confirmation that our faith is not in thought, perception, idea, or hopeless hope. Our faith is grounded in the Bedrock of Truth and reveals to the world that it is real. For the greatest Apologetic argument known to man is to live a holy life. When we live a holy life, which transcends a good life, we reveal to the world that we have the Holy Spirit. The Holy Spirit, in return, reveals to the world that our spiritual side has been transformed and our inner man renewed.

May we always remember that when we become born-again, *"There is* therefore now no condemnation to those who are in Christ Jesus, who do not walk according to the flesh, but according to the Spirit. For the law of the Spirit of life in Christ Jesus has made me free from the law of sin and death" (Romans 8:1-2 NKJV). May we always remember that "those *who are* Christ's have crucified the flesh with its passions and desires. If we live in the Spirit, let us also walk in the Spirit. Let us not become conceited, provoking one another, envying one another" (Galatians 5:24-26 NKJV).

We are who we are because Christ is Who He is. We have become what we have become because of what God has done. When we truly believe, transformation will naturally proceed.

It is "for this very reason, giving all diligence, add to your faith virtue, to virtue knowledge, to knowledge self-control, to self-control perseverance, to perseverance godliness, to godliness brotherly kindness, and to brotherly kindness love. For if these things are yours and abound, *you* will be neither barren nor unfruitful in the knowledge of our Lord Jesus Christ" (2 Peter 1:5-8 NKJV).

May the fruits of the Spirit forever be evident in our lives. For "he who is joined to the Lord is one spirit *with Him*" (1 Corinthians 6:17 NKJV).

May God's Spirit forever lead, change, transform, sanctify, purify, renew, and restore us.

* * *

O God in Heaven, You are the One Who alone transforms man for the better. You alone draw man into Your presence and bring those who once were in darkness into Your Marvelous Light. God, it is in You where everything about life and godliness can be found. Nothing can be received but by way of what Christ has done and by way of the Cross. O God, transform us. Make us new. Keep us from evil and deliver us from temptation. May we see the power of the Cross and the resurrection of Christ. May we receive deeper revelations of what it means to go through the Cross. May we not become distracted by the things of this life, O God. Set our minds on things above. Guide and direct our being as we submit our will to You. We love You, God, and thank You for Your many blessings, promises, and protection. You alone, O God, keep us in the Way, and we thank Thee. In Jesus' name, Amen.

Quotes For Meditation

1. "Jesus Christ, in His infinite love, has become what we are, in order that He may make us entirely what He is." **St. Irenaeus of Lyons**
2. "The Cross is the hope of Christians, the staff of the lame, the comfort of the poor, the destruction of all pride, the victory over devils, the guide of youth, the pilot of mariners, the refuge of those who are in danger, the counsellor of the just, the rest of the afflicted, the physician of the sick, the glory of Martyrs." **John Chrysostom**
3. "Christ is the Artist, tenderly wiping away all the grime of sin that disfigures the human face and restoring God's image to its full beauty." **Gregory of Nyssa**
4. "I do believe we slander Christ when we think we are to draw the people by something else but the preaching of Christ crucified." **Charles Spurgeon**

5. "We must return to New Testament Christianity, not in creed only but in complete manner of life as well. Separation, obedience, humility, simplicity, gravity, self-control, modesty, cross-bearing: these all must again be made a living part of the total Christian concept and be carried out in everyday conduct." **A.W. Tozer**

Chapter 23

Resurrected into Newness of Life

"**F**or as in Adam all die, even so in Christ all shall be made alive." *1 Corinthians 15:22* NKJV

Death is the road to life. Resurrection always follows crucifixion when born-again.

Whatever ceases to be, opens the door to more of eternity. As the floodgates of God's Holy Spirit flow more fully within us, sin slowly dwindles. The path of what could have been apart from Christ is no more. We have power from On High because we have been resurrected into newness of life.

The Cross silences the opinions of man. No one can speak against the Cross of Christ and be deemed as accurate, in the right, or profound.

Anyone who attempts to speak against what Christ did upon the Cross will immediately be brought to shame. Though they may get by for a time with backlashing and scoffing at what He did, God has the final say. God alone has the last word.

Nothing in Heaven or on earth can revert what God has done. In understanding this, we can rest. It is because of Christ that we can change and have newness of life. It is because of Him that we no longer must live our lives earth-bound. Instead, we live for that which is to come. We live for the King of kings and the Lord of lords.

Resurrection is a beautiful transition. It is one where people witness a man who dies beforehand. As they believe that all is lost and forgotten with the man who is crucified with Christ, a beautiful transition takes place before their eyes. There is a coming resurrection that will glorify God and surprise those around.

When we enter newness of life, the radiance of God can be seen from within. Being made in the image of God is no longer covered by a veil but is now a shining Light. The Light of the Holy Spirit shines out the image of God. So much so, that those who see us, speak with us, and interact with us cannot help but see Christ.

Those who live for God do not live for themselves. Those who live in newness of life are not living for the things of this life. "Do not love the world or the things in the world. If anyone loves the world, the love of the Father is not in him. For all that *is* in the world—the lust of the flesh, the lust of the eyes, and the pride of life—is not of the Father but is of the world. And the world is passing away, and the lust of it; but he who does the will of God abides forever" (1 John 2:15-17 NKJV).

Those who do the will of God are not those who work out His Will in the flesh. For nothing can accomplish the Will of God but the Holy Spirit working within. This is why when we are born-again, newness of life brings forth new desires. We no longer attempt to live in the things of this life and the flesh. We no longer feel compelled to have the latest technology, clothing, cars, house, and other externals at the forefront. Instead, our love of the world is not in the things the world produces but in the original beauty that God created it to be.

We begin to focus more on God first, then the creation He has made. We see people as made in the image of God, not as people of a certain color, political party, nationality, or religion. We strive that all would come to know Christ, and we love those who differ from us all the same.

Christianity is not a religion of favoritism. "For there is no partiality with God" (Romans 2:11 NKJV). God is for all and wants all to know Him (1 Timothy 2:4, 2 Peter 3:9). If we have been saved, we can be sure that God desires to save anyone willing to repent of their sins and believe in Christ as the Sole Source of salvation.

"Now in the place where He was crucified there was a garden, and in the garden a new tomb in which no one had yet been laid" (John 19:41 NKJV). When it comes time to die, we prepare ourselves to be laid into a tomb that has not been occupied. Dying and being brought into a tomb that has had many before does not reveal the unique, wonderful, glorious death.

Those who previously died and were brought to the same tombs (or shared the same tombs) did not stand out. Not that they could, because they are dead. "For the living know that they will die; But the dead know nothing, And they have no more reward, For the memory of them is forgotten" (Ecclesiastes 9:5 NKJV). Two people could share the same tomb. One could be wealthy and thriving in the world's eyes, and the other a pauper. Though they were different when alive, they are identical when dead. No one remembers them in the years to come. For people quickly transition to living their own lives. The concern of the deceased is non-existent because they are dead.

Regarding our death, we are buried in a new tomb never used. The reason for this is to reveal the purification of our death. Those who share in tombs are dead and are not expected to rise again. Spiritually speaking, they are bound for Hell and the Lake of Fire. We who are born again are given a new tomb to rest our temporarily dead bodies, for we are not meant to dwell there but to rise again. Just as Christ rose on the Third Day, so we shall be resurrected and rise.

Our tomb is not an end but a means to an End. The tomb signifies that we have truly died, while the new tomb we are buried in reveals that we are children of a higher Kingdom. God declares, "I will be a Father to you, And you shall be My sons and daughters, Says the LORD Almighty" (2 Corinthians 6:18 NKJV). For it is "The Spirit Himself" Who "bears witness with our spirit that we are children of God, and if children, then heirs—heirs of God and joint heirs with Christ, if indeed we suffer with *Him,* that we may also be glorified together" (Romans 8:16-17 NKJV).

Wherever the Holy Spirit is, there is both life and meaning. Wherever the Holy Spirit is not, there is both death and vanity. When we are in a tomb never used, we can be sure that the Holy Spirit is with us.

This significant transition can only occur in the might of His Power! As we rest in our tomb for but a moment, confirming our death, revealing to all that we have truly died, the Spirit descends upon us as a dove. This Heavenly Touch ignites our soul and illuminates our conscience!

We can be sure that we shall never be the same again, for the Spirit of God lives within us. He is the Seal and Confirmation of our salvation. He is the One Who awakens us from our death and draws us into newness of life.

"For if we have been united together in the likeness of His death, certainly we also shall be *in the likeness* of *His* resurrection, knowing this, that our old man was crucified with *Him,* that the body of sin might be done away with, that we should no longer be slaves of sin" (Romans 6:5-7 NKJV). No longer are we slaves to sin, but righteousness. No longer do we pursue selfishness but holiness. No longer are we living for this world but for the one to come!

This new spiritual transformation can only occur when we are resurrected from the death we endured upon the cross. For if we follow in like manner with Christ, we shall also reap what He has provided. If He died, we must die. Since He resurrected, we also shall be resurrected. The old is put off. Behold, the new has come!

As soon as we are resurrected, we come to have both a head knowledge and a confidence within our soul that "our citizenship is in heaven, from which we also eagerly wait for the Savior, the Lord Jesus Christ, Who will transform our lowly body that it may be conformed to His glorious body, according to the working by which He is able even to subdue all things to Himself" (Philippians 3:20-21 NKJV).

One day, we shall be made new and all things will be perfected and purified. No longer will we battle temptation and sin. No longer will we have to continually be on guard and be in need of repenting when we fall. One day, we shall be transformed and conformed into a Heavenly, glorious body. One day, all that is Good, Perfect, and Beautiful shall forever be and continually increase!

Evil and sin will be no more. Sadness and gloom shall never occur. Fear and worry will forever be gone. We will be in Paradise with Him Who died and rose again. We will rule with Him, and we will worship Him.

May we "be filled with the knowledge of His will in all wisdom and spiritual understanding; that you may walk worthy of the Lord, fully pleasing *Him,* being fruitful in every good work and increasing in the knowledge of God; strengthened with all might, according to His glorious power, for all patience and longsuffering with joy; giving thanks to the Father who has qualified us to be partakers of the inheritance of the saints in the light. He has delivered us from the power of darkness and conveyed *us* into the kingdom of the Son of His love, in whom we have redemption through His blood, the forgiveness of sins" (Colossians 1:9-14 NKJV).

* * *

God of Glory, Who gives newness of life to those who repent and believe, fill us with Thy Holy Spirit. May we be brought into Thy Presence, protected from the Enemy, and purified. O God, help us truly die so that we may truly live. May we be found as heirs to Christ. May we be seen as children of the Light. You are Light, O God. You are Life. You offer true freedom to all, Lord Jesus. O God, may we put away all that is not of You. Reveal to us what must go. Give us the strength to seek You and the child-like faith to trust You in all things, for You are the Magnificent One Who loves and cares. You are Him Who gives newness of life. O God, may we walk in the fullness of what Christ has done. Direct our will. Control our mind. Bless our souls. Give rest to our spirit. We receive all that You so graciously give. We thank You for being a God Who is forever beyond all yet sees us. May we forever humble ourselves before You, the God of Heaven and Earth. In Jesus' name, Amen.

Quotes For Meditation

1. "If I had 300 men who feared nothing but God, hated nothing but sin, and were determined to know nothing among men but Jesus Christ and Him crucified, I would set the world on fire." **John Wesley**

2. "The cross of Christ is the true ground and chief cause of Christian hope." **Pope Leo I**

3. "The cross is rough, and it is deadly, but it is effective. It does not keep its victim hanging there forever. There comes a moment when its work is finished, and the suffering victim dies. After that is resurrection glory and power, and the pain is forgotten for joy that the veil is taken away and we have entered in actual spiritual experience the Presence of the Living God." **A.W. Tozer**

4. "The resurrection is the keystone of the arch on which our faith is supported. If Christ has not risen, we must impeach all those witnesses for lying. If Christ has not risen, we have no proof that

the crucifixion of Jesus differed from that of the two thieves who suffered with him. If Christ has not risen, it is impossible to believe his atoning death was accepted." **D.L. Moody**

5. "Preach and live as if Jesus was crucified yesterday, rose from the dead today, and is returning tomorrow." **Martin Luther**

Chapter 24

Suffering is the Road to Glory

"The God of our fathers raised up Jesus whom you murdered by hanging on a tree." Acts 5:30 NKJV

Suffering is the road to glory. So it was with Christ. So it will be with us.

We cannot get to the Kingdom without going through the Cross. We must go through pain to be fully healed. This is not self-inflicted pain, nor is it physical pain. It is an internal pain, for the cross signifies the conviction and death that must happen within (though absolute, physical pain can still arise throughout this life). Anguish, defeat, and times of despair will occur. We will be abandoned and betrayed. This is all validation of our faith. For the road is difficult and the way is narrow. Few there be who find it (Matthew 7:14).

The path of being crucified is one way: God's Way. There is no way around the Cross. There is no alternative. Nothing produced in the flesh is profitable or can lead to that which only

179

comes from God. We can only be led to know God by the path that God has paved.

Only that which comes from God can grow us in God. No external resources can save us. No amount of good works and deeds can get us to Heaven. It is only by Grace through faith (Ephesians 2:8). Therefore, the path to salvation must include crucifixion. This is the only way to truly reveal to God, oneself, and the world that we are willing to live out the true faith. Not merely in words. Not in desire. Not even in action. Crucifixion reveals the greatest aspect of all of us – the intention and motive behind our will.

The Cross tests man's motives and reveals his intentions. One cannot pretend to die and live in newness of life.

Those willing to follow Christ must truly be crucified to be resurrected. Resurrection comes only by way of a true death, and true death only occurs when the motives and intentions are to live for God and to know, love, and serve Him. Without a willingness to deny ourselves, we shall never truly die. We may die partly, but only those truly born-again die in full. Though this full death does not lead to perfection in this life, it is perfect in dying.

A perfect death occurs when one ceases to be their own. A perfect death dies in the hand of God and then becomes filled with God. The Cross, therefore, tests every man and humbles them before God. Those who are unwilling to bend or yield will not truly die. It will be for show and nothing more. Only by having a proper intention can we truly die a perfect death to be filled with the Holy Spirit.

When we suffer, we must wait on God. "But those who wait on the Lord Shall renew *their* strength; They shall mount up with wings like eagles, They shall run and not be weary, They shall walk and not faint" (Isaiah 40:31 NKJV). We tend to want to escape our suffering as quickly as possible when we suffer. We do not want to endure what God Divinely permits and ordains into our lives, even though it is meant for our good — for there is reason in all things when we are following Christ.

We suffer appropriately when we suffer for the sake of Christ and the Gospel. When we endure what has come our way, we do so with the hope of eternal reward. Not that we suffer for the rewards themselves, but we suffer knowing that our reward will be made in full. The hope of Eternity is over the horizon. We continue moving forward and persevering, knowing that all things will pass in this life.

By suffering in this life for the right reasons, we become as Paul in Romans 8:18 (NKJV), and declare, "For I consider that the sufferings of this present time are not worthy *to be compared* with the glory which shall be revealed in us." That which cannot be put into words or imagined awaits us.

As an unbeliever cannot understand what it is to have God's Holy Spirit living in them, we as believers cannot understand what Heaven is like. For we are not there but still bound by our space-time continuum. There is beauty, however, in knowing that a Reality awaits that far exceeds ours. There is an endless ocean of Beauty that is calling us. If we can continually train and reflect on the reality that all saints have had to suffer to reach glory, then we will not feel alone. We will not feel abandoned by God.

Through staying in His Word, we can see that we follow in like manner as the great saints of old. We are in good company, for our suffering is not in vain when we know God. It is for a higher purpose. It is meant to grow, sanctify, and purify us. For "we know that all things work together for good to those who love God, to those who are the called according to *His* purpose" (Romans 8:28 NKJV).

We must, therefore, "not grow weary while doing good, for

in due season we shall reap if we do not lose heart" (Galatians 6:9 NKJV). When our heart is steadfast in doing good to those who persecute and harm us, we reveal God's supernatural Power and Love within us. When we truly desire to do good to all and pray that all might be saved, the suffering that we go through decreases. Our suffering has a purpose; it is meant to draw us closer to glory and invite others to join us. Whether they realize it or not, our doing good to those who hate us gives them undoubted proof that God exists and that we are set apart from this world.

"If your enemy is hungry, give him bread to eat; And if he is thirsty, give him water to drink; For *so* you will heap coals of fire on his head, And the LORD will reward you" (Proverbs 25:21-22 NKJV). We will receive a great reward when we treat our enemies as Christ treats us. Our enemies will not be able to argue against what we have done. They will only fall into a deeper delusion if they do not turn to Christ.

When good is done to those who do evil to us, it is an excellent proof that God is real. It reveals to others that we are not led by how we feel, our emotions, or what people do to us. We remain steadfast in the call of God and do as He commands, despite what is done to us.

"For whatever things were written before were written for our learning, that we through the patience and comfort of the Scriptures might have hope. Now may the God of patience and comfort grant you to be like-minded toward one another, according to Christ Jesus" (Romans 15:4-5 NKJV). Let us learn to be patient amid our suffering. Let us learn to focus on what is to come, not what is current. For whatever is, shall never forever be. All seasons pass. All difficulties dwindle. One day, all things will be made new, and we will be in Heaven with our Lord and Savior, Jesus Christ.

May James 1:12-18 (NKJV) encourage us to continue through all seasons of life:

> "Blessed *is* the man who endures temptation; for when he has been approved, he
> will receive the crown of life which the Lord has promised to those who love Him.
> Let no one say when he is tempted, "I am tempted by God"; for God cannot be
> tempted by evil, nor does He Himself tempt anyone. But each one is tempted when
> he is drawn away by his own desires and enticed. Then, when desire has conceived,
> it gives birth to sin; and sin, when it is full-grown, brings forth death. Do not be
> deceived, my beloved brethren. Every good gift and every perfect gift is from
> above, and comes down from the Father of lights, with Whom there is no variation
> or shadow of turning. Of His Own will He brought us forth by the Word of
> Truth, that we might be a kind of firstfruits of His creatures."

We are all spoken Words of God. We are all image-bearers. For us who are born-again, we hold the Truth, know the Truth, and live by the Truth. Christ is the Truth, and God is a God of Truth. What God has declared, is.

May we focus more on what God has already spoken than what shifting, changing men have to say. May we suffer by way of crucifixion. No matter how painful it may be, our crucifixion will not last. The rising Son is soon to bless us with His Holy Spirit. He will be the Dew within our souls. He will blossom as the flower and will grow as the tree. The Holy Spirit will flow like a river, reminding us that glory will soon come.

May we suffer for the sake of Christ and the Gospel. May we endure the pain and anguish upon the cross as our inner man is crucified. A great reviving will take place — a resurrection we have never seen or experienced within ourselves. The great transition of going through the Cross shall begin, and we will never be the same.

Glory be to God in Heaven for His great promises, undeserved favor, perfect blessings, and great Power of the Holy Spirit coming to live in us and transform us.

* * *

O God in Heaven, Who wills things into existence through His Word, You are King, and we are servants. You are Lord, and we are humans. You are the Ultimate Source of Beauty, Love, and Glory. O God, may we draw nigh to You, knowing that You will draw nigh to us. May we be graced with the willingness to suffer for You. O God, may we never complain about our suffering but see You amid our suffering. As our inner man dies, may we be resurrected and purified. Change us from within, that we may be born-again. Help us to see what lies ahead. May we know that the path to glory is by way of suffering. Be with us, O Great and Wonderful God. Be our Strength and Confidence, Lord Jesus. Be our Advocate and Comforter, Holy Spirit. Be our Protector and Sustainer, Heavenly Father. In Jesus' name, Amen.

Quotes For Meditation

1. "Thus, a godly man wonders at his cross that it is not more, a wicked man wonders his cross is so much." **Jeremiah Burroughs**

2. "When the Christians, upon these occasions, received martyrdom, they were ornamented, and crowned with garlands of flowers; for which they, in heaven, received eternal crowns of glory."
John Foxe

3. "Preach the Gospel. Die, and be forgotten."
Nicolaus Zinzendorf

4. "In every act we do, in every step we take, let our hand trace the Lord's Cross." **St. Jerome**

5. "When someone sets his affections upon the cross and the love of Christ, he crucifies the world as a dead and undesirable thing. The baits of sin lose their attraction and disappear. Fill your affections with the cross of Christ and you will find no room for sin." **John Owen**

Chapter 25

A Promised Hope of Salvation

"Then he said to Jesus, "Lord, remember me when You come into Your kingdom." And Jesus said to him, "Assuredly, I say to you, today you will be with Me in Paradise."" Luke 23:42-43 NKJV

We receive a promised hope of salvation when we go through the Cross. The greatest gift is to be saved from Hell, sin, self, and all evil. Greater still, the promised hope of salvation allows us to know, grow in, love, and understand more about our Creator. It gives us the ability to live for God and to know God.

What child is born that does not want to know their parents? What child enters life wanting to live by themselves?

Naturally, we are personable beings. We are freewill agents created in the image of God. Every child that enters this world desires to know their parents. This child-like wonder and curiosity is beautiful, but sadly it does not last. As many grow, they lose their curiosity of life, purpose, meaning, and interest in seeking answers to deeper questions.

Many want to live for themselves and seek fulfillment in that which God creates rather than God directly (Romans 1:25). This terrible situation is what leads to idolatry, discontent, and unfulfillment. Many become unsatisfied because they raise the means over the Ultimate End. Since God cannot be surpassed, He is the Ultimate Basis of all things. He is the Endless Pursuit of our soul. Though man can exalt and place ahead of God things within his own misguided will, God remains the Bedrock and Ground of all Reality and Truth.

"For the wages of sin is death, but the free gift of God is eternal life in Christ Jesus our Lord" (Romans 6:23 NKJV). If God has declared that the way to eternal life is through Christ, then this is Truth. It is not some idea or belief that is not grounded in reality. This notion that we are saved only by and through Christ is based upon evidence, facts, truth, and God Himself.

Christ is God. He is One of the Three in the Trinity. Therefore, what God declares is the way of salvation is, in fact, true. It does not matter what mere man thinks. It does not matter that many will attempt to have us believe that God's Way is "not the way".

Whatever man seeks to destroy within us or deviate us from, we must not give way. For God offers salvation to all, and He wants all to come to the knowledge of Him (1 Timothy 2:4).

When people are willing to humble themselves before God, they can be raised into newness of life. As we die on the Cross and are resurrected, we can be sure that we have gone through the Cross. The work is finished. We have entered into newness of life. We have received a promised hope of salvation. No longer is it an invitation from God, but it is now a reality that shall be lived. The Holy Spirit seals us. We now continue in righteousness, godliness, and holiness.

"My sheep hear My voice, and I know them, and they

follow Me. And I give them eternal life, and they shall never perish; neither shall anyone snatch them out of My hand. My Father, who has given *them* to Me, is greater than all; and no one is able to snatch *them* out of My Father's hand" (John 10:27-29 NKJV).

It is easy to tell who knows God by how they live. Multitudes speak but do not act. Many act but do not believe. Some believe, but not in Truth. They believe what Christ has done but don't believe in His call for us to change, submit, and surrender our lives to Him. Therefore, those who hear God's Voice and respond and act to His Voice truly know God, for they do not conform God and His Word to fit their needs. Instead, they conform their lifestyles to match His Immutable Word and Truth.

"For it pleased *the Father that* in Him all the fullness should dwell, and by Him to reconcile all things to Himself, by Him, whether things on earth or things in heaven, having made peace through the blood of His cross" (Colossians 1:19-20 NKJV). Christ has provided the Only Way to Eternal Life. He is the reason for us being changed and transformed.

When we go through the Cross, we become a different creature. We are renewed and restored. We are sanctified and changed. We now walk into all that God has offered. We have been given the hope of eternity. All that we were no longer remains. Day by day, we shed off that which is not of God and take up all that is of God.

This is the beauty of having a promised hope of salvation. We no longer must live in guilt and shame. We no longer must cover up or attempt to hide what is wrong. When we mess up and sin, we repent and confess our sins. We know that God is not some harsh master in the sky who is out to destroy and damn us. He is a loving God Who is willing to forgive us of our sins and discipline us. For salvation is not merely the door that opens us up to eternity but also to have the Kingdom of God reign within at our present moment (Luke 17:21).

When we have received the promised hope of salvation, we receive God's gifts, blessings, and promises. All He offers and gives is not merely for the life to come but for this life.

Salvation can change the trajectory of our life here and now. We don't need to wait for the life to come. Instead, we can do now what will bring a sampling of Heaven while in this life.

People need to know Jesus. Not the Jesus created by man, but the Jesus Who is truly Lord and Savior. People need to see the love, care, and compassion of Jesus. People need to hear of the holiness, justice, and wrath of God. God must be portrayed to the world. When we spend time in the Word, having been given the hope of salvation, we become better equipped to share the Truth in love.

Salvation brings forth many blessings. A man may be full of knowledge, but he is nothing without that knowledge challenging and transforming him. 1 Corinthians 13:1-13 (NKJV) declares:

> "Though I speak with the tongues of men and of angels, but have not love, I have
>
> become sounding brass or a clanging cymbal. And though I have *the gift*
>
> *of* prophecy, and understand all mysteries and all knowledge, and though I have all
>
> faith, so that I could remove mountains, but have not love, I am nothing.
>
> And though I bestow all my goods to feed *the poor,* and though I give my body to
>
> be burned, but have not love, it profits me nothing. Love suffers long *and* is kind;
>
> love does not envy; love does not parade itself, is not puffed up; does not behave
>
> rudely, does not seek its own, is not provoked, thinks no evil; does not rejoice in
>
> iniquity, but rejoices in the truth; bears all things, believes all things, hopes all
>
> things, endures all things. Love never fails. But whether *there are* prophecies, they
>
> will fail; whether *there are* tongues, they will cease; whether *there is* knowledge, it
>
> will vanish away. For we know in part and we prophesy in part. But when that
>
> which is perfect has come, then that which is in part will be done away. When I was

a child, I spoke as a child, I understood as a child, I thought as a child; but when I

became a man, I put away childish things. For now we see in a mirror, dimly, but

then face to face. Now I know in part, but then I shall know just as I also am

known. And now abide faith, hope, love, these three; but the greatest of

these *is* love."

By going through the Cross, those who have the promised hope of salvation can obtain all that Christ offered and is willing to give. We can receive God's gifts and use them for His glory. We can love with true, Biblical love. We can learn to endure all and love the Truth, no matter how convicting it may be. For "The way of a fool *is* right in his own eyes, But he who heeds counsel *is* wise" (Proverbs 12:15 NKJV).

Those willing to listen to God and yield all they are to Him shall receive all that God desires to give — not in the want of using God as a means, but in serving Him as an End. For all that is from God is meant to be used to serve God.

Therefore, those who receive the hope of salvation must endure to the very end. Going through the Cross is not a one-time act that dictates the rest of our lives. It is an initial act that reveals the heart's disposition for the rest of our life. "For you have need of endurance, so that after you have done the will of God, you may receive the promise" (Hebrews 10:36 NKJV). The promised hope is for those who endure.

Those who truly go through the Cross are dedicated to the call of God and the path that must be taken. Though some are to fall away, for we know that "the Spirit expressly says that in latter times some will depart from the faith, giving heed to deceiving spirits and doctrines of demons" (1 Timothy 4:1 NKJV), those willing to persevere shall receive the promise. They shall receive the gift of eternal life.

As long as time permits, perseverance, steadfastness, and endurance are necessary. For they are the proof and sign that we are genuinely saved. Anyone can claim the faith and leave the faith. Those who truly believe in the faith will live out the faith. They will work out their salvation with fear and trembling (Philippians 2:12).

This can only be done when the power of the Holy Spirit is living through us. "For though He was crucified in weakness, yet He lives by the power of God. For we also are weak in Him, but we shall live with Him by the power of God toward you. Examine yourselves *as to* whether you are in the faith. Test yourselves. Do you not know yourselves, that Jesus Christ is in you?—unless indeed you are disqualified" (2 Corinthians 13:4-5 NKJV).

Let us live in the finished work of the Cross by going through the Cross, being promised the hope of salvation, and living in the power of the Holy Ghost. We can do this in confidence because "the love of God was manifested toward us, that God has sent His only begotten Son into the world, that we might live through Him" (1 John 4:9 NKJV).

May all come to live under the finished work of Christ's crucifixion and resurrection.

* * *

O Blessed Savior, You have given us everything pertaining to life and godliness. May we never forget all that You have done for us. May we never work against the Truth, but do all things for the Truth. May we live in the finished work of the Cross, knowing that our sins have been forgiven. O God, bless us with more power from Your Holy Spirit that we might not sin against Thee. Strengthen us in Thy Love. Guide and direct our steps. May we see You in all things and know that You are forever with us. Thank You for the transformation that is taking place. May we go through the Cross with complete assurance that we are saved.

Touch us, O Holy Spirit, and uplift our souls. May we operate based upon the promised hope of eternity so graciously given to us. Keep us from distraction and enticement. Help us to love all, Holy Spirit. We ask for Your blessing, Heavenly Father, that we may bless others. Be glorified, O God of all. In Jesus' name, Amen.

Quotes For Meditation

1. "How sweet it is to die if one has lived on the Cross!" **St. John Vianney**

2. "Is it a small thing in your eyes to be loved by God - to be the son, the spouse, the love, the delight of the King of glory? Christian, believe this, and think about it: you will be eternally embraced in the arms of the love which was from everlasting, and will extend to everlasting - of the love which brought the Son of God's love from Heaven to earth, from earth to the cross, from the cross to the grave, from the grave to glory - that love which was weary, hungry, tempted, scorned, scourged, buffeted, spat upon, crucified, pierced - which fasted, prayed, taught, healed, wept, sweated, bled, died. That love will eternally embrace you." **Richard Baxter**

3. "Now let the Heavens be joyful, Let earth her song begin; Let the round world keep triumph, And all that is therein; Invisible and visible, Their notes let

all things blend, For Christ the Lord is risen, Our joy that hath no end." **St. John of Damascus**

4. "Without Easter, Good Friday would have no meaning. Without Easter, there would be no hope that suffering and abandonment might be tolerable. But with Easter, a way out becomes visible for human sorrows, an absolute future: more than a hope, a divine expectation." **Hans Urs von Balthasar**

5. "Gospel preachers nowadays preach the gospel of the Crucifixion, the Apostles preached the gospel of the Resurrection as well. The Crucifixion loses its meaning without the Resurrection. Without the Resurrection the death of Christ was only the heroic death of a noble martyr; with the Resurrection it is the atoning death of the Son of God. It shows that death to be of sufficient value to cover our sins, for it was the sacrifice of the Son of God." **R.A. Torrey**

Part Six

Taking Up Our God-Appointed Cross

Chapter 26

Taking Up Our God-Appointed Cross

"We must bear our crosses; self is the greatest of them all. If we die in part every day of our lives, we shall have but little to do on the last. O how utterly will these little daily deaths destroy the power of the final dying!" Francois Fenelon

A God-appointed cross always brings purpose and meaning, and the suffering that must be endured is meant to grow, stretch, mold, and shape us into the image of Christ.

Anything that God brings our way or permits that is difficult is always met with a beautiful intent and ending. If we are willing to endure what God has brought our way, we shall reap a harvest beyond what we can comprehend. The fruits of this harvest may not be evident in this life, but they will most certainly be revealed in the next. "The end of a thing *is* better than its beginning; The patient in spirit *is* better than the proud in spirit" (Ecclesiastes 7:8 NKJV).

Our toughest cross to bear is the continual denial of self.

The more we deny self, the easier life becomes. When we cease worrying about our wants, desires, and comfortability, it becomes easier to endure pains and persecutions. When we no longer see ourselves as deserving of anything but the suffering that happens, we can bear our cross with a smile.

Those who see themselves as nothing are those who receive everything. Not nothing in their being, but nothing in worthiness. We are not worthy or deserving of anything. We are all worse sinners than we realize. Nonetheless, when we are born again, we know we are seen as royalty in the family of Christ. This royalty includes promises to be recognized but should not influence prideful change within our hearts. Instead, it should bring confidence in knowing who we are in Christ.

Seeing ourselves as deserving of God's blessings is to live in pride and neglect of dying to self. Seeing ourselves as deserving nothing from God opens up the floodgates to a pure, humble disposition of the heart to receive God's blessings. If we are willing to die to any inclination that boosts the ego of what we think we are, then we shall bear all things and reap all things. We shall not be bound by our delusion that we deserve a free, easy, happy life.

Though there are times of receiving these in different seasons, this life involves adversity. "In the day of prosperity be joyful, But in the day of adversity consider: Surely God has appointed the one as well as the other, So that man can find out nothing *that will come* after him" (Ecclesiastes 7:14 NKJV). Only those who are real with themselves shall be grounded in mind with what occurs in life.

May we learn to take up God's appointed cross for our lives. Let us see ourselves as nothing and die to self, daily. In doing so, the end will be an easy death and transition, for we are not holding onto anything in ourselves or this world. Our one desire is to be with God.

As we have died to all that is not God and not of God, we prepare ourselves for a hopeful and peaceful transition. Those who learn to take up their God-appointed cross shall willingly endure all trials, understand that their adversity does not equal what Christ went through, submit to the Will of God continually, and deny any rights they believe or perceive they have.

May God be glorified as we embark, carry out, and endure all He brings our way, permits in our lives, and gives to us. For He is the Omniscient and Sovereign Lord Who loves us, cares for us and does what is contrary to our wants so that we may receive what we need.

Blessed be the Holy Name of the Lord Jesus Christ.

Chapter 27

Willingly Enduring Trials

"**M**y brethren, count it all joy when you fall into various trials, knowing that the testing of your faith produces patience. But let patience have its perfect work, that you may be perfect and complete, lacking nothing." James 1:2-4 NKJV

A God-appointed cross is never in vain, so long as it is endured with eyes set upon God and a request of His strength and grace to see us through.

We cannot partake in what God Divinely orchestrates without His assistance. We cannot be men who are conquerors without God at the forefront and within us. We can only endure trials that come our way through a willingness, and in this willingness comes the flow of the Holy Spirit. As He takes control, we learn the spiritual fruit of patience. We learn to wait for God to deliver us from that which God has permitted.

Life is an act of giving by God, for God. We, as vessels, merely reap what He gives. For nothing we own or possess is from us. God gives to men all. It is "God the LORD, Who created the heavens and stretched them out, Who spread forth the earth and that which comes from it, Who gives breath to the people on it, And spirit to those who walk on it" (Isaiah 42:5 NKJV).

When we learn to see that God gives all, we can better endure the trials that come. We don't see them as random events that might lead to a better outcome. We don't linger in the hope of being delivered from the trial. Rather, we rest in the knowledge of Him, Who called and loved us. We continue in the way, knowing that The Way is with us. He has allowed our faith to be tested so that we might grow in patience.

Patience is one of the most difficult spiritual disciplines. Aside from humility, it may be the most difficult to build because we want what we want when we want it. Very few of us are willing to suffer for the sake of Christ. Yes, many of us claim it in words, but when trials come our way, we quickly complain. We lose sight of Who God is and quickly idolize the trial we are going through.

Whatever pain, suffering, adversity, or difficulty we face, we tend to overemphasize what is going on. Everything around us becomes heightened and deemed as worse than it is when we do not willingly endure the trial that has come. When we look upon our circumstance rather than Him Who has permitted the circumstance, we quickly complain, become agitated, and are put in a distressful state. As this happens, we lose sight of the reality that God shall deliver in His time.

By our complaining, we can even endure our season longer than we could have otherwise.

God permits trials to strengthen our faith. When we are strengthened in our faith, we possess greater patience — patience for those who wrong us. Patience for those who perse-cute us. Patience for petty trifles in relationships. Patience in waiting for a new job. Patience in understanding God's Will. Patience with rebellious children. Patience with bitter and resentful co-workers. Patience with long lines. Patience with indecisive people. Patience with the way that things are. No matter what comes our way, agitation and irritation dwindle when patience increases.

What used to affect us – whether big or small, relational or conceptual – no longer takes hold of us. The things that used to bother us now appear as petty. They have no hold on us, for we are wiser. The testing of our faith through trials opens our perspective and allows us to see God's Faithfulness and Sovereignty be displayed in our lives. For if trials never came our way, the proof of God's Faithfulness would never be revealed.

It is easy to praise God in the easy times but difficult to praise Him in the difficult times. Though God's Faithfulness is always at work, it is often seen and proven by what we must endure. If we willingly endure God's appointed cross for our lives, we shall lack nothing. We shall reach a state of greater perfection. We shall grow in righteousness through sanctification. As we are changed, we are more prepared for the next level in the faith. Our growth will bring forth patience, and our patience will produce greater faith.

Anyone who endures a trial on behalf of Christ and sees God's Faithfulness at work shall have more faith in the days ahead. When trials continue to increase in quantity and difficulty, we shall be more readily prepared than we were a decade ago.

We can be as Paul and declare, "But in all *things* we commend ourselves as ministers of God: in much patience, in tribulations, in needs, in distresses, in stripes, in imprisonments, in tumults, in labors, in sleeplessness, in fastings" (2 Corinthians 6:4-5 NKJV). We can reach a point where we are satisfied in our response toward adversity because we have been trained to be patient and wait upon the Lord. We no longer perpetually complain. Instead, we see these are crosses we must bear for the sake of Christ, ourselves, and others.

For the sake of Christ, we grow in the knowledge of Him. For the sake of ourselves, we learn to die to self and wholly trust God. For the sake of others, we know how to reveal the truthfulness of our faith and the power of the Holy Spirit. For it is only by God that we can show God to the world. Sometimes, the greatest way to do this is by remaining at peace as we endure trials, having our confidence in God alone.

Amid our suffering, we must not be quick to demand to get out. We must not cry that Christ would come merely to deliver us from our God-appointed cross, for some people desire Christ's return not because they want to see Christ but because they want to escape their suffering (not knowing that their suffering is God's appointed cross for them to bear).

To cry out to God to be instantly delivered from what God has appointed or permitted is to lack faith and lack willingness and want to live for Him. Of course, we all go through different trials in various degrees, at various times, and in various ways. It is easy to speak on this, but it is tougher to live it out. Though this be true, it is important to be reminded that God has His reasons which we know not. We must trust in Him with childlike faith and surrender, for the fruits of enduring suffering far exceed the ease of instantly being delivered.

This is our promise through Christ: "eternal life to those who by patient continuance in doing good seek for glory, honor, and immortality" (Romans 2:7 NKJV). We seek after these things because these things are from God. We continue to do good, despite others afflicting and hurting us. We learn not to be resentful or bitter toward others. Rather, we learn to die to how we feel, what we want, what we think, what we desire, what we think we deserve, when we think things should happen, how we think things should happen, our vision for our life, our dreams, our motivations, our perspectives, our want of ease, and our selfish fulfillment.

We learn to continue doing good in the name of Christ so that we might receive immortality in Heaven. For glory and honor are God's, and we are to reveal that glory and honor in how we conduct ourselves. Those who can continue on in God's appointed cross shall receive a blessing beyond what could be given by never going through difficulty.

May we never become discouraged or fearful in the way of righteousness. For Him Who was and is Righteousness had endured much suffering. If Christ our King went through the most horrific, tormenting death, can we not bear a little uncomfortable pain for His Name's sake?

Let us learn to "glory in tribulations, knowing that tribulation produces perseverance; and perseverance, character; and character, hope" (Romans 5:3-4 NKJV). Our hope is not unwarranted, and our character transformation in Christ is not in vain. If we learn to persevere, we shall portray more of Christ to the world. Why? Because more of Christ both lives and is active within us.

May our hope not be in being delivered in our time and in our way. Instead, may our hope be in the promised growth in virtue, conduct, faith, and service to God.

Not many are deemed worthy to carry a God-appointed cross. Only the strongest in desire for God and willingness to serve Him in all regards shall be given greater crosses to bear. These may not always come in the form of depletion in health, sickness, or losing a loved one. Sometimes, the greatest crosses are through spiritual warfare and persecution from the world.

If we learn to willingly endure all trials for the sake of God and His Glory alone, we shall reap an eternal reward. This can only come from the hand of God.

May we learn to endure all things for the sake of Christ. For "God demonstrates His own love toward us, in that while we were still sinners, Christ died for us" (Romans 5:8 NKJV).

May we grow in the faith by the testing of our faith, for this is the path of patience and perseverance. This is how we grow in character, having a proper hope in God alone to both deliver us, grow us and have His way in us. May He give us the strength to press on until we are called Home.

* * *

Heavenly Father, Him Who possesses all things, You alone bring what we do not want to make us into what we cannot do on our own. You alone give meaning and purpose to all things. You alone are our Strength and our Song. You alone are worthy of praise in all seasons. You alone are Faithful. You alone are Good. You alone care for all individuals. O God, may we learn to willingly endure all trials to glorify Your Name. Give us the strength to turn to You and see You through all our seasons. May we not give way to the flesh but be alive in the Spirit. O God of Glory, write a new story upon our hearts. May we be a burning fire that others are attracted to. May we burn with Holy Ghost fire, that others may be drawn to us and see Christ in us. May we carry ourselves in a Christlike manner in all situations. Blessed Savior, teach us Your ways. Grow us in the faith. We set our eyes and hope on You, the Great and Mighty Deliverer. In Jesus' name, Amen.

Quotes For Meditation

1. "What are you to us, you who are cut off from God, a fugitive for Heaven, and a slave of evil? You dare not do anything to us: Christ, the Son of God, has dominion over us and over all. Leave us, you thing of bane. We are made steadfast by the uprightness of His Cross. Serpent, we trample on your head." **Seraphim of Sarov**

2. "You must accept your cross; if you bear it courageously it will carry you to Heaven." **St. John Vianney**

3. "Life is wasted if we do not grasp the glory of the cross, cherish it for the treasure that it is, and cleave to it as the highest price of every pleasure and the deepest comfort in every pain." **John Piper**

4. "The passion of Jesus is a sea of sorrows, but it is also an ocean of love. Ask the Lord to teach you to fish in this ocean. Dive into its depths. No matter how deep you go, you will never reach the bottom." **Paul of the Cross**

5. "To take up the cross of Christ is no great action done once for all; it consists in the continual practice of small duties which are distasteful to us."
John Henry Newman

Chapter 28

Understanding Our Adversity Does Not Equal What Christ Went Through

"Therefore, my beloved brethren, be steadfast, immovable, always abounding in the work of the Lord, knowing that your labor is not in vain in the Lord." 1 Corinthians 15:58 NKJV

As we do the work and will of God, we will go through adversity.

There will be times when we desire to quit, don't feel like continuing on, question God, and wish we could get out of doing what needs to be done. These feelings and states come from our emotional, fleshly side. Of course, emotions are good to have. God has emotions. He reveals His love, tender-kindness, wrath, disappointment, and joy throughout Scripture. However, the difference between us and God is that our emotions tend to lead us. For God, His emotions are based upon His Nature and are always congruent with Who He is. They are always in the right because God is always in the right.

When our emotions lead us, we tend to refrain from enduring. Rather than seeing our trials with our spiritual eyes, we see them with our fleshly eyes. When this occurs, we tend to be bound to the present rather than looking ahead and pressing on.

Sadly, when things are good, we tend to look ahead at what we do not have and neglect to see how good things are in the present. Our flesh always mixes our understanding. Our flesh always gets in the way of enjoying our current season or seeing the profitability within each season.

Whatever the adversity to come, we must see Christ. If life seems too difficult, we must remember Him upon the Cross. Soon, our problems will disappear as we compare our trials to His sufferings. For our adversity does not measure up to the sufferings of Christ, for He went through the worst pain imaginable. Not only was He tortured and tormented; not only was He falsely accused and His reputation (in its perceived state from others) brought down; He was crucified on the Cross, and The Heavenly Father forsook Him.

In this life, we can always run to the Father because the Father forsook Christ. We may have earthly fathers who abandon us, betray us, fail to take care of us, and are merely blood relatives who are not active in our lives. God the Father, however, is Perfect and Pure. No matter who our earthly father is, only One Father truly loves unconditionally. It is because of Christ being forsaken that we can enter the loving hands of our Heavenly Father.

Comparing God to what we know can be such a travesty. Deception is afoot when God is seen based upon the neglect and misrepresentation of others who claim His Name.

Satan has twisted the minds of many to base Christianity on *a* person rather than *Thee* Person. The Enemy has made others see the Heavenly Father like their earthly father. This misguided view has led many away from the faith. Amid this, people don't see God as loving and having sent the Perfect Lamb to be slaughtered by His creation. By neglecting to see the love of Christ upon the Cross, they fail to enter the faith through the Cross. However, those of us who are born-again have understood the Love of God and the Holiness of God. We know what truly happened upon the Cross.

Christ upon the Cross demonstrated all that God is, all that He desires, and all that He is willing to both do and give. God's desires, of course, are satiated and fulfilled in Him alone. Nonetheless, His desire for us to come and know Him remains. He has done all the work. He merely waits for us to come forth into His Divine Presence.

When Christ was forsaken by the Father, He took on the full blow of God's wrath. Many may see Samson as the strongest in the Bible, but it was Christ, for only One could take on the entire weight of man's sin. Only One could receive the entire blow of God's wrath and be resurrected. It was the Perfect God-man, the Lord Jesus Christ.

When we see that we are entirely responsible for sending Christ to the Cross, we will bear our difficulties with more understanding. When we see that we deserve nothing, we will more willingly endure that which God has appointed.

We should be humbled when we compare our temporal pains and sufferings to Christ's, for no one has ever endured what Christ had to endure. Though mockers and scoffers may say that it was only a few hours of pain, they do not understand the spiritual battle that took place. They do not understand how High and Holy God is. They would be less inclined to ridicule what Christ has done if they understood such realities. If they were not so prideful, they would see the humility and love of Christ. For no man of high status would come down to the level of a pauper and give his life for theirs.

"Then they compelled a certain man, Simon a Cyrenian,

the father of Alexander and Rufus, as he was coming out of the country and passing by, to bear His cross" (Mark 15:21 NKJV). When we bear our God-appointed cross, we also help bear Christ's. Not in a *literal* sense, but in a *metaphorical* sense. We become a friend of Christ, walking alongside Him. We are willing to be part of Christ and show the world that we are close to Him. Whatever the world may say or think, we would rather carry the cross than continue to live as one who is lost.

"Many are the afflictions of the righteous, but the LORD delivers him out of them all" (Psalm 34:19 ESV). Whatever we go through, God permits it to grow and test us. This test is not out of spite or entertainment. This test is out of love and helps us reveal to ourselves that we are nothing and that all strength comes from God. It gives us the opportunity to turn to Christ and see that what we are going through cannot compare to what He went through. If we will humbly and patiently persevere and endure that which God has appointed in our lives, it allows God to be God in our lives.

"For it has been granted to you that for the sake of Christ you should not only believe in Him but also suffer for His sake" (Philippians 1:29 ESV). We are called to suffer for Christ's sake. For the path of suffering is the path that leads to glory. The way of adversity is the way of the cross.

Affliction and persecution are two proofs that we are in the one, true faith. Any form of Christianity that does not go through struggle and difficulty, both spiritually and externally, is not a true faith. No one ever made it to Heaven by way of a hammock. All men and women make it to Heaven by way of the Cross of Christ.

Whatever we are to suffer for the sake of Christ is always less than what He endured. Never will we take on the same amount of pain and anguish as Christ. Though our weight may be heavy, His was heavier. Though our spirits may be crushed,

His was forsaken by the Father. Whatever is to come, we must always see outside ourselves and look to Christ.

We must reflect on what He went through. We must get our eyes off ourselves and look to the Glory to come. One day, we will be set free from adversity. For now, may we continue to press on in the vapor of time we have in this life. For one day, all things will cease to be. No longer will we endure pain, but only prosperity with God Almighty.

"But may the God of all grace, who called us to His eternal glory by Christ Jesus, after you have suffered a while, perfect, establish, strengthen, and settle *you*. To Him *be* the glory and the dominion forever and ever. Amen" (1 Peter 5:10 NKJV).

* * *

O God of Beauty, Who brought Heaven down to us that we might come to know Heaven above, may Yours be the Kingdom, the Power, and the Glory forever. You alone are Love, God. By You, we can love. By You, we can come to know You. O God, whatever comes into our lives, help us reflect on Christ. Help us go to You in all humility, seeking Your assistance and aid. You alone are the Great Physician and Deliverer. We can do nothing without You. We can endure nothing without You. O God, how we need You in all things, in all ways, at all times, and in all places. Bless us with more of Your Holy Spirit. May He Comfort us in our adversity. May He empower us to persevere and allow our season to grow and stretch us. No matter the pain, may You be glorified. If You were willing to suffer for us, Lord Jesus, how can we neglect to suffer for You? Keep our eyes, minds, understanding, and thoughts forever on the truths of You and Your Word. Crucify us, that we may be sanctified, purified, and perfected. In Jesus' name, Amen.

Quotes For Meditation

1. "However much we suffer for the love of Jesus Crucified, it is but little." **Benedict Joseph Labre**

2. "Whenever anything disagreeable or displeasing happens to you, remember Christ crucified and be silent." **St. John of the Cross**

3. "A cross borne in simplicity, without the interference of self-love to augment it, is only half a cross. Suffering in this simplicity of love, we are not only happy in spile of the cross, but because of it; for love is pleased in suffering for the Well Beloved, and the cross which forms us into His image is a consoling bond of love." **Francois Fenelon**

4. "Allowing yourself to be put in such a position that God is exalted is the goal of living the crucified life. When you allow God to be exalted in your difficulties, you will be in the perfect position to smell the sweet fragrance of His presence." **A.W. Tozer**

5. "The road is narrow. He who wishes to travel it more easily, must cast off all things and use the cross as his cane. In other words, he must be truly resolved, to suffer willingly, for the love of God in all things." **St. John of the Cross**

Chapter 29

Submitting to the Will of God

"Rejoice always, pray without ceasing, in everything give thanks; for this is the will of God in Christ Jesus for you." *1 Thessalonians 5:16-18 NKJV*

The will of God is that in all seasons, we would seek Him, trust Him, believe Him, and give Him glory.

In all things, we are to submit to God. This submission is not based on doing as we are told merely because we are told. God does not want us to submit to Him because He is desirous to rule over us in such a way as many have done before us, for many of us have come from difficult homes. Fathers and mothers wanted us to submit to them in *everything*, not *everything that was good*. Many of us have had bosses that made us do things that we knew were contrary to the best interest of all individuals. We all know a coach, teammate, teacher, or friend who has wanted us to submit to them without question and pushback.

Sadly, many base submission to God in a similar fashion

when this occurs. Prior experiences with fallen, finite creatures tend to wrongly dictate the viewpoint of the Perfect, Infinite God. When this happens, a carnal rebellion seeps into our being.

Though this rebellion has always been, this rebellion is enhanced when we hear anything about submitting to the Will of God. We quickly tense up and feel not only discomfort but anger. Due to our prior experiences with humans, we become much more guarded and angered when we are told that God wants us to submit to His Will.

This should not be the case, for the Will of God is easy for those who seek it and know God. God's Will is never forced. It can sometimes be difficult to persevere in His Will, but it is easy to understand. God does not require us to obey the 613 commandments, as the Jews continue to practice. Instead, He requires simplicity in our externality and holiness internally. These two wings are what God desires, for everything flows from them (to understand more about simplicity and holiness, see my book, **Two Wings**).

With simplicity and holiness in mind, we can be sure that the will of God is to grow us in these. Sometimes, our season will be filled with prosperity. Other times, our season will be filled with adversity. Whatever the season, we must trust that the Will of God is being forwarded amid what we are currently going through. "In the day of prosperity be joyful, But in the day of adversity consider: Surely God has appointed the one as well as the other, So that man can find out nothing *that will come* after him" (Ecclesiastes 7:14 NKJV).

We never know the end of a thing, only its beginning. For we are all beginnings that have yet to experience the end of God's Will.

God's Will is not only an initial creation but a continued

sustainment. God's Will is not only an Immutable decree but includes diversity and variation within the unchanging decree.

God's Will for our lives, collectively, is the same. Individually, however, His Will is differentiated for each of us (though the end is the same), for He desires all to come and know Him and repent of their sins (1 Timothy 2:4, 2 Peter 3:9).

In taking up our God-appointed cross, we die to our will. In following the call of God for our lives, we submit and surrender all to Him. In everything, we must give Him thanks, for God owns everything. We own nothing. God rules over all. He is the One Who knows what is always best. He knows what must be done in its perfect timing. He knows what must be allowed to further us along the path of godliness. He alone is All-Wise.

Knowing this, we can truly submit to God in everything. No matter how painful, we know there is a blessing on the other side. For every birth is painful in the beginning but brings forth an incredible blessing. Likewise, when we become born-again, we can expect times of pain in this life. However, this will not remain. One day, either in this life or without a doubt in the next, we shall live in God's blessing. His presence will be forever with us. He will not leave us on the road of adversity. Instead, He commands us to submit to Him (James 4:7), give thanks to Him in all things (1 Thessalonians 5:18), and He shall take care of the rest. For He is the Great Deliverer, the One in Whom we trust.

When our heart, soul, and mind are in sync with submitting to the will of God, we shall be as John and declare, "He who has the bride is the bridegroom; but the friend of the bridegroom, who stands and hears him, rejoices greatly because of the bridegroom's voice. Therefore this joy of mine is fulfilled. He must increase, but I *must* decrease. He Who comes from above is above all; he who is of the earth is earthly and speaks of the earth. He Who comes from heaven is above all" (John 3:29-

31 NKJV). God must forever increase in our lives. Not from His standpoint but from our exaltation of Him.

"As many as desire to make a good showing in the flesh, these *would* compel you to be circumcised, only that they may not suffer persecution for the cross of Christ. For not even those who are circumcised keep the law, but they desire to have you circumcised that they may boast in your flesh. But God forbid that I should boast except in the cross of our Lord Jesus Christ, by whom the world has been crucified to me, and I to the world" (Galatians 6:12-14 NKJV). If our focus is on God, we shall not desire the things of this world. They may tempt us, but we will not give into them, for we see that submitting to God's Will is of the most significant importance and greatest reward.

As a prodigy who listens to his master is rewarded, so are we by God. Not that we fall psychologically prey to following Him only because of the blessing, but because we are glorifying Him Who is higher than any leader, president, or king.

Many will brag and speak about famous people they have met, but what about bragging that we know the Lord? We speak so highly of individuals and neglect to do so with God that it is no wonder we are miserable. Our hope and excitement come from man, not God. Our desire to share with others famous people we have met, but not God, is idolatry. This can only be combatted when we continually put God at the forefront and seek and submit to His Will.

"For Christ did not send me to baptize, but to preach the gospel, not with wisdom of words, lest the cross of Christ should be made of no effect. For the message of the cross is foolishness to those who are perishing, but to us who are being saved it is the power of God" (1 Corinthians 1:17-18 NKJV).

The world will scoff and mock that we follow a crucified Savior. This, however, is where our power comes from! For the message of the Cross of Christ has power and glory. It should lead us to live for Him in all things and trust Him with all things. For God's "Divine power has given to us all things that *pertain* to life and godliness, through the knowledge of Him Who called us by glory and virtue, by which have been given to us exceedingly great and precious promises, that through these you may be partakers of the divine nature, having escaped the corruption *that is* in the world through lust" (2 Peter 1:3-4 NKJV).

The promises of following God and His Will lead to an abundance of all things that pertain to life and godliness. For life can be lived without experiencing Life Himself. Only Him Who is Life can give life to our lives. True life is to live in the Will of God. This, in return, brings forth godliness.

As we submit to God, more of God becomes active within us. As we cease striving to do as we desire, we become more sensitive to His prompting and speaking. When we spend more time in the Word than in worldly books, we become more sensitive to the Voice of the Holy Spirit. As we hear more of the Spirit, we discern God's will and what is good and acceptable (Romans 12:2).

Let us see our God appointed-cross as a means to grow in God. As we submit to the Will of God, our adversity gains weight and meaning. For sorrow, affliction, and death all have a greater meaning and purpose when we are born-again believers. When we submit to the Will of God, we do not trust in ourselves. Instead, we trust in God.

Whatever we submit to has our energy, time, heart, and trust. If we submit to the Will of God, then it shall be God Who helps us complete His Will. If we do not submit to the will of God, we place our trust in ourselves to get through what we have brought about to ourselves. This is a dangerous path and one that leads to destruction. However, those who submit to God's Will shall always have spiritual peace.

Though our hearts may become perturbed by what is occurring, we have this quiet confidence that God is with us. We see our God-appointed Cross as a means of significant growth and maturing. We understand that true beauty is found in the cross. Just as in Christ, all things unfold; so, at the cross, all things embark on a beautiful transition.

May we seek to always live in the Will of God. May we submit to God in all ways. For the more we do so, the easier it becomes. The easier it becomes, the more God's Will shall be fulfilled and furthered throughout our lives. We will not grieve the Holy Spirit (Ephesians 4:30) or quench the Holy Spirit (1 Thessalonians 5:19). Instead, we will truly take up our cross and follow Christ into all that God has for us, has prepared for us, and desires us to go through.

Thanks be to God, that we do not have to endure anything alone. We don't need to ""worry about tomorrow, for tomorrow will worry about its own things. Sufficient for the day *is* its own trouble"" (Matthew 6:34 NKJV). For God has declared that we ""Be strong and of good courage; do not be afraid, nor be dismayed, for the LORD your God *is* with you wherever you go"" (Joshua 1:9 NKJV).

May we submit to God's Will during adversity in the same manifestation that we are willing to accept times of prosperity, for He knows the end of a thing from its beginning because He declared the end from the beginning (Isaiah 46:10). He truly is "the Alpha and the Omega, *the* Beginning and *the* End, the First and the Last" (Revelation 22:13 NKJV).

May God be glorified in all we do, say, and think. Let us "not be foolish, but understand what the will of the Lord is" (Ephesians 5:17 ESV). May we pray to God that His Kingdom come and that His will be done on earth as it is in heaven (Matthew 6:10 NKJV).

Blessed be the name of the Lord.

* * *

Heavenly Father, Great are You, and Mighty are Your works. You are Wonderful, Beautiful, and Gracious. You are Kind and Loving. You bring purpose in adversity and grow us in all seasons. You genuinely love us and care for us. O God, may we grow in You continually. May we learn to endure all seasons for Your glory. May we trust that You are for us and not against us. Holy Spirit, give us the active faith that continually meditates on God, for we know that You are Him Who is above all and oversees all. You are the One Who knows the end from the beginning. You are the One, O God, in Whom we can put our trust and hope. For You will never leave nor forsake us. Your rod and staff comfort us. You are Perfect, O God, and we submit to Your Word, Your Will, and Your Wisdom. Direct our paths and make them straight. Bless us with perseverance. May we enjoy every season and see You in it. We give thanks to You, O God, in everything. For all things have a purpose when we are found in You. In Jesus' name, Amen.

Quotes For Meditation

1. "The suffering of adversity does not degrade you but exalts you. Human tribulation teaches you, it does not destroy you. The more we are afflicted in this world, the greater is our assurance for the next. The more we sorrow in the present, ..the greater will be our joy in the future." **St. Isidore of Seville**

2. "Glory follows afflictions, not as the day follows the night but as the spring follows the winter; for the winter prepares the earth for the spring, so do afflictions sanctified prepare the soul for glory." **Richard Sibbes**

3. "When we grow careless of keeping our souls, then God recovers our taste of good things again by sharp crosses." **Richard Sibbes**

4. "Under the influence of fear, we bear the Cross of Christ with patience. Under the more inspiring influence of hope, we carry the Cross with a firm and valiant heart. But under the consuming power

225

of charity, we embrace the Cross with ardor." **St. Bernard of Clairvaux**

5. "Entrust yourself entirely to God. He is a Father and a most loving Father at that, Who would rather let heaven and earth collapse than abandon anyone who trusted in Him." **Paul of the Cross**

Chapter 30

Denying Any Rights

"I have been crucified with Christ; it is no longer I who live, but Christ lives in me; and the life which I now live in the flesh I live by faith in the Son of God, Who loved me and gave Himself for me." Galatians 2:20 NKJV

Taking up our God-appointed cross involves the death of self. It consists in dying to what we think is owed to us and what we deserve.

Those who hang onto misguided illusions that the world owes them will not be dead to the world. They will not be those who are merely *in* the world; they will be those who are also *of* the world. They will be those who think that because they are made in the image of God, they deserve to be treated as "gods". Even if they do not recognize the truth that they are created in the image of God, they still live as if they have the right to request anything, and it should be given to them.

Anything an individual requests is either good or bad; it is either sound or unbalanced. Whatever a person believes they have the right to, that very thing can be a benefit, idol, or hindrance. Most times, due to our polluted souls, we pervert that which we request. Even in our request for rights, we pervert the request by seeking rights that are ungodly, un-Biblical, and foreign to Heavenly nature. These requests and rights tend to be parameters that we want to be set up so that we may live as we want.

The natural state of man is not upright but sinful. Ever since the Fall, men have demanded their rights. They have stood up for the right to have rights. Yet, our Father in Heaven commands us to deny our rights.

When Paul states that he is crucified with Christ, he dies to all he is. He dies to the very notion that his body is his own and he has the right to do whatever he wants with his body. Those who think they can do whatever they want with their own body have failed to see God as the Creator of their body. Without God, they would not be; they could not be. Without God, there is no us. Without God, we would not have our souls implanted into our bodies.

God is the Creator of all. We did not choose to come into this world at a specific time. We did not decide who our parents were, where we would be born, what we would look like, the color of our skin and hair, the height we would come to be, and all other properties given to individuals. We did not choose our personality, voice, or vessels. We are who we are because God is Who He is. He created us in His image.

Sadly, those made in His image distort that image. For us who are born-again, there is a daily fight against the flesh and being crucified with Christ. Those who are unconverted distort God's image without any care in the world. How is this done? By living for themselves and demanding their "rights".

Those who demand their rights will never deny their rights.

This is the differentiation between many self-proclaimed Christians from born-again believers.

Many will demand that they have the right to do such and such, but those who are crucified with Christ will deny their rights. They will want to put to death all they are and all they thought they were apart from Christ. They will not desire to hang onto that which is ungodly. They will not want to seek rights that will "provide" them the ability to sin without consequence. They will not want to be "god" in their lives. Instead, those who deny their rights can accept all God has for them, for there are no barriers, constraints, or limitations for those who are found in Christ and deny themselves daily.

People think freedom is being able to do anything, but true freedom is found in doing the right thing. True freedom is not free, unless it is found in God. True freedom is found in restricting our self-will, self-governance, and self-righteousness. Freedom is found in being crucified with Christ so He may live through us.

Of course, there is always an ongoing battle between the flesh and Spirit. "For the flesh lusts against the Spirit, and the Spirit against the flesh; and these are contrary to one another, so that you do not do the things that you wish" (Galatians 5:17 NKJV). This battle, however, is good. It proves that there is a war within us. There is a desire to do right but a lack of strength to carry it out. Unless the Holy Ghost is with us, we shall never combat our fleshly desire to demand "our rights". Instead, we will continually demand them.

Even Paul had this great struggle between the flesh and the Spirit. His war was between what he wanted to do and what he did. We hear of his great battle within himself in Romans 7:15-25 (NKJV):

"For what I am doing, I do not understand. For what I will to do, that I do not practice; but what I hate, that I do. If, then, I do what I will not to do, I agree with the law that *it is* good. But now, *it is* no longer I who do it, but sin that dwells in me. For I know that in me (that is, in my flesh) nothing good dwells; for to will is present with me, but *how* to perform what is good I do not find. For the good that I will *to do,* I do not do; but the evil I will not *to do,* that I practice. Now if I do what I will not *to do,* it is no longer I who do it, but sin that dwells in me. I find then a law, that evil is present with me, the one who wills to do good. For I delight in the law of God according to the inward man. But I see another law in my members, warring against the law of my mind, and bringing me into captivity to the law of sin which is in my members. O wretched man that I am! Who will deliver me from this body of death? I thank God—through Jesus Christ our Lord! So then, with the mind I myself serve the law of God, but with the flesh the law of sin."

The war of our will is not an excuse to idle and be taken over by our want (or lack thereof). The war of our will is to continually seek God for deliverance and strength in carrying our God-appointed cross.

Only God can give our inward man the strength to deny our demand of rights to live as we choose, as we please, as we think fit, as we believe is right, and as we desire. Only God can free us from self and make us lively in the Spirit.

Just as Paul waged war with himself, he did not always succumb to his fleshly self. He did not make excuses and complain about how difficult the war of the will was. No, he fought against his carnality daily. Though there were times of falling, Christ lived more greatly in him and Paul saw victory. He was a new person. He became a different creature. He went from killing Christians to becoming one. Only the power of the Holy Spirit can change a man to think and do as such.

Likewise, we must find our strength in God alone. We must admit that we shall fall on this progressive road with Christ. However, this admission does not give us the right to think we have the right to sin.

Those who are truly born-again seek freedom *from* sin, not freedom *to* sin. They desire to be set apart and detached from the world, the flesh, and everything contrary to God. When they sin, they repent. They don't claim, "Well, everyone has their weaknesses. Everyone is a sinner. God will always forgive me." They do not use God's Grace as lasciviousness, for we know that "certain men have crept in unnoticed, who long ago were marked out for this condemnation, ungodly men, who turn the grace of our God into lewdness and deny the only Lord God and our Lord Jesus Christ" (Jude 1:4 NKJV).

Rights are not externals demanded by our internal state. Rights are not that which comes *to* us but that which comes *from* us (as exercised on a Biblical basis). We don't have the right to demand from others what we want them to bow to. We don't have the right to receive whatever we want. We don't even have the right over ourselves. God owns all because He created all. The sooner we recognize this, the more excellent victory we will have in our Christian walk, and the more the Holy Spirit will be active within us.

"I speak in human *terms* because of the weakness of your flesh. For just as you presented your members *as* slaves of uncleanness, and of lawlessness *leading* to more lawlessness, so now present your members *as* slaves *of* righteousness for holiness" (Romans 6:19 NKJV). We are called to be slaves of righteousness.

This is the irony of being a slave to God – it is where freedom is found. In denying our rights, we increase in righteousness.

We can only be upright when we cast down our rights. We can only be righteous through the Blood.

Being covered by the Blood includes us denying our rights. When we go to the Cross, we demand nothing from God. In demanding nothing, we receive everything. In humility, we accept responsibility for our sins. We do not seek to go around the Cross, obtaining some Heavenly benefits without the call to die. No, we choose to be transformed by the power of the Cross of Christ and His resurrection.

O Saints of God, may we see that God is Good. May we understand that we have no rights of our own. We have nothing to demand of God, only to receive what He is so graciously willing to give. We have earned nothing. We deserve nothing. We are sinners saved by Grace through faith (Ephesians 2:8-9) when we believe Jesus Christ is Lord and Savior and repent of our sins.

Our new birth brings Life and Light. The Love of God manifests within, and we are resurrected into the Body of Christ. When this occurs, we live our lives for God in the power of God. We live by His Word and Truth. We become slaves to Him.

In being slaves to righteousness, we are free. Not free to do as we please, but free to worship, serve, love, know, and follow God. In doing so, the weight of everything contrary to God is lifted. We experience a spiritual transformation within. Through this beautiful change, our soul begins to blossom. We are no longer our own but God's. We now live for a higher calling. We live for a higher purpose with more significant meaning.

Let us never prolong the process of our sufferings and adversity due to an unwillingness to yield to God's Will, Way, and Word. Let us trust that as we take up our God-appointed cross, we will be sanctified and purified. We shall not give way to our fleshly desires that claims we are deserving. Rather, we patiently endure our seasons of affliction and strife just like the saints of old.

This life is not the end. We shall not die in torment. We shall not cease to exist, having nothing to gain for our endurance. God shall reward us abundantly if we patiently see that all of God's crosses are meant to make us more into the image of His Son.

May God be with us throughout all of our days. Only He can give us the strength to accomplish what He has called us to do. Only God can make us holy by His Holy Spirit.

May God forever receive Glory and Honor for His willingness to be with us, stretch us, grow us, and patiently wait for us to turn to Him. The war shall forever wage. Adversity shall come. Pain will occur, but in the end, the reward shall be great. For ""he who endures to the end shall be saved"" (Matthew 24:13 NKJV).

May "the God of all grace, who called us to His eternal glory by Christ Jesus, after you have suffered a while, perfect, establish, strengthen, and settle *you*. To Him *be* the glory and the dominion forever and ever. Amen" (1 Peter 5:10-11 NKJV).

* * *

Triune God, You are Him Who rules and reigns supreme over all. You are High and Lifted Up. You are the Great Alpha and Omega. You are the Ancient of Days. In You are all Truth and Light. You give life to every man and woman. You love those You created in Your image. You are Holiness and Righteousness. O God, may we die to any inclination that we deserve anything. Give us the strength, O Holy Spirit, to deny our rights. May we see that freedom is found in being Your slave. For in being Your slave, we shall be Your friend. Those who desire to serve You shall forever live with You. God, we know that You are not a hard taskmaster. We know that You love us and are calling us to higher ground. We know that You are a God of blessing. God, we acknowledge that we have no right but to do the Will of You

Who made us. O God, keep us on the straight and narrow. May we never steer to the left or right, but forever keep our eyes fixed on You. We look straight ahead and press into Your promises, for You alone are Good, O God. We carry our God-appointed cross given to us by You, willingly. May we endure to the end and receive all You have for us. We love You, God, and we are thankful for the opportunity to grow in You and be made more like Your Son. In Jesus' name, Amen.

Quotes For Meditation

1. "I live in a world that demands its rights. I live a faith that commands me to deny every one of them." **Paul Washer**

2. "The cross is not a mere event in history; it's a way of life! Take up your cross DAILY, Jesus said!" **John Piper**

3. "God afflicts us because He loves us, and it is very pleasing to Him when in our afflictions He sees us abandon ourselves to His paternal care." **Benedict Joseph Labre**

4. "There is no better wood for feeding the fire of God's Love than the wood of the Cross." **Ignatius of Loyola**

5. "We can add to our God-given cross by agitated resistance and an unwillingness to suffer. This is simply an evidence of the remaining life of self." **Francois Fenelon**

Conclusion

"For Jesus Christ I am prepared to suffer still more." St. Maximilian Kolbe

The Way of the Cross is difficult. It tests the heart and mind. It chastises the will and the soul. It purifies the conscience and spirit. It is a brutal, long road that few venture down.

Even those who venture to the Cross are tested when they arrive at the Cross. For the Cross is the Pillar of Truth. It is the crossroads that cross-examines the heart and calls us to die.

For those of us who do not fear crucifixion, we shall receive a promised resurrection. The old self will be slaughtered and the new self will be put on. For the Cross is the way that leads from a sinful life to a sanctified life; a wretched heart to a pure heart; a corrupt soul to a holy soul; a wicked mind to a righteous mind. Only by the Cross of Christ can we be transformed into children of the Light. Only by the Cross can we die to all that is ungodly and be redeemed and restored into godly saints.

As St. Anthony of Padua once said: "The Devil is afraid of

us when we pray and make sacrifices. He is also afraid when we are humble and good. He is especially afraid when we love Jesus very much. He runs away when we make the sign of the Cross."

The Cross symbolizes the defeat of sin, self, the world, carnality, iniquity, Hell, death, the Devil, and his legion of demons. The Cross is the beautiful image that reminds us of the Perfect Blood that was shed by Him Who is Holy and Pure.

The mystery of what was done on the Cross continues to expand as we progress down the Righteous Road. Revelations of what happened on the Cross become more known as we press into God continually.

May we desire that all would come to understand and walk in *The Way of the Cross*. May all decide to take up their cross, go to the Cross, arrive at the Cross, hoist their cross, and be nailed to their cross that they might go through the Cross and experience newness of life. For this is the only way to a Heavenly transformation. This is the only path that leads to everlasting life and coming to believe, know, and live for Him Who is Life.

The Cross is the way. We must be willing to submit and surrender all to God if we are to be raised and brought into the family of God.

God's transformative power, saving grace, and Divine Love is offered to all, but the testing ground is met at the Cross. "For Jews request a sign, and Greeks seek after wisdom; but we preach Christ crucified, to the Jews a stumbling block and to the Greeks foolishness, but to those who are called, both Jews and Greeks, Christ the power of God and the wisdom of God. Because the foolishness of God is wiser than men, and the weakness of God is stronger than men" (1 Corinthians 1:22-25 NKJV).

God's Way is right, whether we accept it or not. The world

may disagree with what God has declared. They may fight It on all sides. They may attempt to get around It, pervert It, add to It, take away from It, or ignore It. No matter the feelings or perceptions of man, God offers salvation to all. His Immutable Way shall forever be the Way, so long as He is the Way.

Let us learn to walk in *The Way of the Cross*. May we gain deeper revelations of the Cross of Christ, for this is the way to a blessed, fulfilling, purpose-filled, strengthened, new, hopeful, joyful life.

For us who become born-again, we can be as David in Psalm 91:1-16 (NKJV) and declare the promises that are given to us:

"He who dwells in the secret place of the Most High Shall abide under the shadow of the Almighty. I will say of the Lord, "*He is* my Refuge and my Fortress; My God, in Him I will trust." Surely He shall deliver you from the snare of the fowler *And* from the perilous pestilence. He shall cover you with His feathers, And under His wings you shall take refuge; His truth *shall be your* shield and buckler. You shall not be afraid of the terror by night, *Nor* of the arrow *that* flies by day, *Nor* of the pestilence *that* walks in darkness, *Nor* of the destruction *that* lays waste at noonday. A thousand may fall at your side, And ten thousand at your right hand; *But* it shall not come near you. Only with your eyes shall you look, And see the reward of the wicked. Because you have made the Lord, *who is* my refuge, *Even* the Most High, your dwelling place, No evil shall befall you, Nor shall any plague come near your dwelling; For He shall give His angels charge over you, To keep you in all your ways. In *their* hands they shall bear you up, Lest you dash your foot against a stone. You shall tread upon the lion and the cobra, The young lion and the serpent you shall trample underfoot. "Because he has set his love upon Me, therefore I will deliver him; I will set him on high, because he has known My name. He shall call upon Me, and I will answer him; I *will be* with him in trouble; I will deliver him and honor him. With long life I will satisfy him, And show him My salvation.""

God will protect us through all. He will be with us through all. He will comfort us through all. He will see us through all. For safety is in the Lord, and He will direct our paths. He will give us the strength to take up our God-appointed cross with cheerful hope, knowing that we are being trained, sanctified, and strengthened in the faith.

We can take up our God-appointed cross, knowing it is not in vain, for all things that come from God have meaning and purpose. If we endure our God-appointed cross willingly, we shall receive God's blessing eternally.

May God forever be at the forefront of our lives as we seek to serve Him.

Let us close with the wonderful words of Martyn Lloyd-Jones:

> "Are you glorying in the cross? Is this everything to you? Is this life to you?...Your eternal, everlasting destiny, depends upon this one thing. Have you seen that God has provided there, the only way whereby you can be forgiven and become a child of God, and go on to inherit the glories of eternity? May God have mercy upon us all, and by His Spirit open our eyes to see the glory of the cross."

Afterword

I appreciate you taking the time to read through **The Way of the Cross**. I hope it benefited your growth in understanding what it truly means to take up your cross and follow Christ and what will happen as you progress in *The Way of the Cross* of Christ.

If this was a blessing, it would be greatly appreciated if you took a few minutes to write a review on Amazon.

An honest review can go a long way and help make the book more visible to future audiences.

If you feel led to do so, I truly do thank you.

Judah Veritas

Author

Let's Connect

If you would like to connect with Judah Veritas, you can find him on the following platforms:

For All Relevant Social Media, Linktree: https://linktr.ee/judahandjackieveritas

For Judah's Services: https://stan.store/ascendwithveritas

About Judah Veritas

Judah Veritas came to a more profound knowledge of God when he realized it was only Jesus Christ Who could break the chains of sin that kept him bound.

He is passionate about diving deeper into the study of Who God is, His Attributes, His Nature, and His Being, and sharing the revelations he has received with all who have an ear to hear. His desire is for others to know God intimately. Not only as Father, Son, and Holy Spirit, but as Creator of the Universe.

His testimony is impactful, as it reveals God as the Deliverer. He was supernaturally set free from an addiction to pornography and masturbation at age 23, as a Non-Denominational Christian, and received the gift of tongues and discerning of spirits upon getting married.

Since the age of 25, Judah has consistently posted one

video each day on YouTube containing apologetic, theological, or philosophical insight. He is an Entrepreneur, dedicated Author, and husband to his wife, Jackie Veritas.

Also by Judah Veritas

Judah has multiple books in the works expected to launch this year and the years ahead.

The Way of the Cross is his third book, alongside his first and second books, *Ineffable Attributes* and *Unraveling Deception*. Others that are expected to come pertain to God (His Nature and Being), the importance of the inner life as a Christian, the way of a true born-again believer, his personal testimony, and much more.

One of the books to be released soon that was mentioned throughout The Way of the Cross is the following:

- *Two Wings (pg. 226)*

Be sure to stay in touch with his social for updates on upcoming books. Some of these include:

- *The Unknown Known*
- *The Forever Unknown*
- *The Inner Life*
- *Absolute Supremacy*

We hope *The Way of the Cross* was an edifying read that benefited your growth in understanding what Christ did upon the Cross and how we are to follow in like manner.

God bless you, keep you, guide you, and continue to lead you in His Will, according to His Word.